*To my husband Scott whose love and support
have given me the wings to take flight.*

A CALL
to
DELIVER

Tom Monaghan, Founder of Domino's Pizza,
and the Miracles and Pilgrimage
of Ave Maria University

Peggy Stinnet

Clovercroft Publishing

A Call To Deliver: Tom Monaghan, Founder of Domino's Pizza
and the Miracles and Pilgrimage of Ave Maria University

©2015 by Peggy Stinnet

Published by Clovercroft Publishing, Franklin, Tennessee

Cover and Interior Design by Suzanne Lawing

Editing by Bob Irvin

Printed in the United States of America

978-1-942557-08-1

WHAT PEOPLE ARE SAYING ABOUT
A CALL TO DELIVER

This is a fascinating story of a man on a mission, driven by his faith in God's providence and love. Living in a secularized culture often critical of religious beliefs, Tom Monaghan is an exemplar of a faithful servant who is true to his church and dedicated to the evangelization of God's people, especially the young. With the founding of Ave Marie University, Tom Monaghan leaves a great legacy of one who came from humble beginnings, built a successful business enterprise and now shares the fruits of his labors by giving his life and resources in the service of others. He truly fulfills the mandate of Christ to love God and neighbor.

ADAM CARDINAL MAIDA
ARCHBISHOP EMERITUS OF DETROIT

Anyone who has wondered how Tom Monaghan became the Catholic Church's leading equipper of lay apostolates must read this book. Monaghan's extraordinary success at Domino's Pizza tells us how he got the funds. It doesn't tell us the personal, social and spiritual influences that enabled him to take a rich man's vow of poverty and use his fortune to start, support and then, turn loose apostolates as diverse as Legatus, Ave Maria University, Ave Maria School of Law, Thomas More Law Center, Ave Maria Communications and many, many others. Peggy Stinnet's story of Monaghan's unlikely life provides a window on his spirituality and love of the Church. The Call to Deliver is also rich with testimonies and reminiscences from those who have known, worshipped and worked with him through the years. No other book offers as appreciative a look into the life of one of American Catholicism's most fruitful disciples of Christ.

AL KRESTA, PRESIDENT AND CEO, AVE MARIA COMMUNICATIONS. HOST, "KRESTA IN THE AFTERNOON."

Talk about Power From the Pews! Peggy Stinnet's meticulously researched saga of a modern day spiritual Horatio Alger leaves the reader breathless with the extent of the miracles wrought by one man's conversion. Tom Monaghan's road from rags to spiritual riches should inspire all with eyes to see what God can do with hearts willing to use the gifts the Creator has given them as He intended those gifts to be used.

PEGGY STANTON, AUTHOR, COLUMNIST.
RADIO HOST, "POWER FROM THE PEWS,"
"ORDER OF MALTA" AND "MINUTES WITH THE
CATECHISM."

A book that delivers the behind-the-headlines, quiet, religious man that Tom Monaghan truly is.

MICHAEL NOVAK, TEMPLETON PRIZE
LAUREATE 1994

This book is dedicated to those who followed this Godly vision and ventured out to these former fields in Southwest Florida to build something that would be eternal. They are the faculty, staff, students, Founders and pioneers who have made this dream a reality.

I would also like to thank Tony Zollo who has selflessly shared with Ave Maria University his talent of photography over many years and has taken many of the photos enclosed in this book.

Most especially I would like to thank Tom Monaghan for following the Will of God to bring souls to heaven through this endeavor and the many other initiatives that he began which have produced good and lasting fruit.

It is with heartfelt thanks that we must also express gratitude to God for the gift of Our Blessed Mother whose presence and guidance has always been with us and to whom we are consecrated. Ave Maria!

INTRODUCTION

After Tom Monaghan, the founder of Domino's Pizza and Ave Maria University, finished his first book, *Pizza Tiger*, many thought that he should write a follow up book since the ending left the reader wondering what happened next. Tom's closing statement in Pizza Tiger ended with these words;

> *"My point, as I close this final chapter, is that I believe there is something in life that's a lot bigger and more important than Domino's. I have faith that God will help me find it and that He'll show me the way to my ultimate goal which is to go to heaven and take as many people as possible with me."*

Since *Pizza Tiger*, Tom Monaghan has had the opportunity to reassess his life. From the time he was a young boy in the orphanage he always thought big, but for many years it was about acquiring things and impressing people. As the founder of Domino Pizza, Inc., his company dominated the pizza delivery market and was doing $3.5 billion in sales when he sold it. Through Domino's he achieved many of his boyhood dreams by owning the Detroit Tigers and winning a World Series, but now the question is… *was this all luck or a greater plan of God's?*

Throughout history God has accomplished great things by using small and simple ways. A few fish and loaves, the water jars at Cana, and His call to fishermen to "come follow me." Jesus even used the simple substances of bread and wine to perform His greatest miracle by transforming them into His own Body and Blood. These are all examples that show us that we are never too small to be used by God; in fact, it is a requirement to holiness. In becoming little we "decrease" so he can "increase" (John 3:30) so we like Mary, can give our own "yes" where God can begin to plant in us new seeds of hope to be carried out into the world.

Long before that first shovel hit the ground in the lush tomato fields of Southwest Florida in what would someday be the university and town of Ave Maria, God had already begun His work of hope and restoration by calling to pilgrimage all those who could hear the sound of His voice. It was His plan, His vision that He be born again in the hearts of men and carried out to all segments of our society that were withering without His presence. Economics, education, politics, medicine, and especially the family were being scorched and choked out by the weeds of an anti-God that worshiped at the altar of indifference, secularism, and an atheistic world view. This was especially true in higher education, where many of our young people were being formed and taught that it was better to believe in nothing than to follow Christ. But God, who is the true vine and the antidote to a dying world, was already pruning and cultivating those whom he had set aside for this particular task of saving souls.

While Tom Monaghan's *"rags to riches to rags"* story is far from small or simple, God was ready to use him to build something eternal that countless others could also be a part of. Blessed, broken, set apart, and shared, many were being called to be part of this great miracle. For those who have been part of the journey, this road, like that of Calvary, has not always been an easy one; however, Jesus promised us that if we even had faith as small as a mustard seed that *nothing is impossible* (Matthew 17:20). It was on that seed the promise that Ave Maria was built, but not just with brick and mortar in these former fields, but in the hearts of those who captured this Godly vision.

CHAPTER ONE

Million Dollar Baby

"I will not leave you as orphans, I will come to you."
JOHN 14: 18

"He's worth a million dollars."

Those were the prophetic words that Francis Thomas Monaghan spoke when he saw his son for the first time on March 25, 1937. Thomas (Tom) Monaghan said because of his Irish heritage his parents were probably hoping that he was born on March 17, St. Patrick's Day, but he was glad to be born on this day, because, being pro-life, what he eventually came to understand was that next to Easter, this was the second-most important day of the year, even more important than Christmas. This was the Feast of the Annunciation, the day when the Angel Gabriel announced to Mary, "Hail Mary," or in, Latin *"Ave Maria,"* and that she would become the Mother of Jesus, the Son of God. It was at the moment she responded, "May it be done to me according to thy Word," and the Holy Spirit overshadowed her, that Christ became truly present, because it is at conception that a child really enters the world, while birth is just a change of location.

Tom Monaghan's journey in faith began at the age of four, when his father died at the age of 29 on Christmas Eve in 1941 from peritonitis caused by chronic ulcers. He has wonderful but short memories before then as a young boy of following his father doing chores and going to Mass on Sunday with him, his mother Anna (Geddes), and younger brother Jim at St. Thomas the Apostle and St. Patrick's Church in Ann Arbor. His mother Anna was a Lutheran convert, something that was expected at that time. While he has some recollections of saying the traditional meal and nighttime prayers, he says he remembers little else, accept that they were a family.

Following his father's death Tom and Jim, who was only two at the time, were placed in foster homes because of their mother's meager income and her difficulty in raising two young boys while also attending nursing school. The plan was she would come back for them when she finished school and could afford it, but as it turns out it was a very long time before they were a family again.

In 1943, at the age of six, his mother placed the boys in St. Joseph's Home for Boys in Jackson, Michigan. Tom recalls Jackson was also home to the largest prison in the United States and, for him, St. Joe's made that two! St. Joseph's was very strict and everyone had a number. His number was 25, but he didn't mind, because that was Hal White's jersey number; White was a pitcher for the Detroit Tigers. At St. Joe's the boys all had chores, from mowing the lawn to polishing the floors and doing laundry, but Tom was often given the great honor of cleaning the chapel. He said he can remember spending hours in that chapel, which he now believes gave him a great respect for the Eucharist. Looking back, he can see how this time spent with Jesus has had a great impact on his faith.

Living in the orphanage, run by Polish Felician sisters, all the boys were immersed in the faith. Each day there would be Benediction and Mass and they would say long morning and evening prayers together as well as recite the rosary. Weekly they would receive the sacrament of confession. In their religion classes they learned the Baltimore Catechism, memorizing all the questions and answers in it over the years. "Who made you?"- *God made me.* "Why did God make you?" - *To know, love, and serve Him in this world and to be happy with him in the next.* "What is sanctifying grace?" - *Sanctifying grace is that grace that makes the soul holy and pleasing to God as long as we are not guilty of mortal sin.* While these doctrines were instilled in his mind as a young boy, they would later rest in his heart and become the spiritual compass of his life.

Tom can remember making his First Communion in the second grade at St. Joe's wearing the same white knickers, shirt, and tie that were worn by all the boys and kept tidily packed away by the sisters in the attic to be used each year. It was about this same time that he first considered the priesthood, something that he said all the boys thought about, maybe because of their strong religious upbringing, but also because there were no girls around to influence the decision. In the fifth grade he made his Confirmation and took the name of Joseph. In the orphanage they had no other choice but were all given the name Joseph. Since Tom lost his own father at such an early age, he liked the name because that was the name of the foster father of Jesus, so he thought it was a good one.

While he was at St. Joseph's, Tom was fortunate enough to have one of the very best teachers, who he said was like a mother and father to him. In the first and second grade Sr. Mary Berarda, who was only in her mid-twenties at the time, had the patience of a saint and was a kind and nurturing woman. She was someone who he responded to and who always encouraged him even when his ideas seemed rather farfetched. Tom told his classmates once that when he grew up he wanted to be a priest, an architect, and a shortstop for the Detroit Tigers. While the other kids laughed and said it was impossible to be all three, Sr. Bereda responded with, "Well, I don't think that has ever been done before, Tommy, but if you want to do it there is no reason you can't." That became Tom's inspiration to aim high in life and, prophetically, he did come close to achieving many of those boyhood dreams. The amazing impact that this one sister had on him in growing in his faith during these formative years and throughout his entire life would be something that he would always remember, and motivate him later to become involved in Catholic education. Sr. Berarda passed away at the age of 65 in 1983, but before she died, and after learning Tom bought the Detroit Tigers, he received a beautiful letter from her that was written in the perfect Palmer method, and they were able to make contact again.

Oddly enough, Tom's mother lived only blocks away from the orphanage the entire time Tom and Jim were there. After finishing nursing school she would walk by St. Joe's every day to get to her job at the nearby hospital and sometimes visit on Sundays or take the boys out but Tom said it always felt strange knowing that he was living in an orphanage when he was not an orphan at all. Looking back he could see that his mother was trying to do her best, to provide for her boys a good home and a Catholic upbringing, but as a child this was difficult for him to understand.

Finally in 1949, at the age of 12, Tom's dreams of becoming a family again finally came true. His mother took a job as a nurse in the small northern Michigan town of Traverse City, about 250 miles north of Ann Arbor. Traverse City has some of the most beautiful scenery imaginable, surrounded by orchards and the pristine waters of Lake Michigan and, for Tom, after being in the strict discipline of the orphanage, the total freedom was exhilarating. In Traverse City he attended Immaculate Conception school and church and the boys met the pastor, Fr. Russell Passeno (later ordained a Monsignor), who would also have a huge influence on Tom's life. From the very beginning Fr. Passeno was encouraging to him and a wonderful role model, a lot like Sr. Berarda. He served mass as an altar boy at Immaculate Conception, and Fr. Passeno gave him odd jobs to do around the school and church for 35 cents an hour, knowing Tom's eagerness to work but also aware of his family situation. Tom was in the seventh grade at the time but would later attend St. Francis High School only a few miles away.

Tom's goal was to get a job right away, so he went up and down the main street in town looking for one. He wanted to get a paper route with the local daily paper, the *Traverse City Record Eagle*, but they gave him a corner hawking papers instead in front of Milliken's department store at Front and Cass. He would sell about thirty papers a day, hollering,

"Record Eagle, tonight's paper!" The papers sold for five cents and they made two cents on each one, returning any unsold papers for a refund.

One day, while selling his papers, he saw a beautiful frosted crystal statue of the Madonna in the window of Martinek's Jewelry Store, across the street from where he sold his papers. It cost a whopping $7.50, which added up to a lot of papers, but Tom bought it anyway as a Christmas gift for Fr. Passeno. That Christmas almost every penny Tom made went towards presents for Jim, his mother, and Fr. Passeno, but he said it really felt good to be able to buy those gifts and saw it as a fun spending spree. Fr. Passeno was extremely delighted when he offered him the Madonna and later, after his death, the statue that Tom gave him as a young boy still stood proudly on his desk along with a letter Tom wrote him. Tom now has it on a shelf in his home to remember this kind and holy man who was such an inspiration to him.

The summer following seventh grade, Tom got a job picking cherries with a boy named Paul Steffes. Picking cherries was hard and tedious work, and Tom remembers thinking the business should make a machine that would shake the trees and catch them in a tarp to be more efficient which is, of course, the way they do it today. He also remembers doing a lot of fishing with Paul that summer on Grand Traverse Bay and then selling their catch door to door. He was always thinking of some way to make a buck.

Unfortunately, Tom continued to have a lot of problems with his mother, and their troubles only seemed to worsen, so she applied to the state's Children's Home and Aide Society to have he and Jim placed in foster homes once again. One option was to live on a foster farm, an idea that Tom found appealing. He thought he would like living on a farm, being outdoors and doing chores and caring for the animals as he once did with his dad. Jim was also sent to a foster farm, but he moved back in with their mother after only a short separation.

The first farm Tom was placed in was owned by a man named Johnson who lived on North Long Lake Road just outside of Traverse City. The only problem was there wasn't much of a farm left. The barn was empty and there were no animals or cows to milk. After six months he went to live on the Beaman farm near Interlochen, just south of Traverse City, but Mr. Beaman wasn't farming either. His barn was torn down and there was only one cow left, which Mr. Beaman milked himself. However, Mr. Beaman had a gravel pit on a lot nearby and Tom was able to help him with loading and deliveries. While living there Tom attended the Interlochen School, which was a public two-room schoolhouse, where he graduated from the eighth grade. When he did occasionally return to Traverse City, he spent as little time home as possible but remembers instead playing a lot of ping-pong in the basement of another friend, Alan Gray.

ALAN GRAY: BOYHOOD FRIEND OF TOM MONAGHAN'S FROM TRAVERSE CITY

I met Tom Monaghan during the seventh grade at Immaculate Conception School shortly after he moved to the Traverse City area. We were both altar servers, which most of the boys were at that time, and taught by the Sisters of Mercy, who were not very merciful. There were four classrooms in the school with two grades in each, and approximately twenty-five students to each room. Later we would also attend St. Francis High School together where I remember the principal, Sr. Roberta, being a pretty decent person, all 4'8" of her, but it was pretty comical for her, and us, when she tried to discipline boys that were now 6 feet tall.

Fr. Passeno, the pastor at Immaculate Conception, was a very friendly and considerate man—who understood that Tom needed friends and made the suggestion that we invite him over for a game of ping-pong or the other things that boys did at that time. He and his brother Jim had a very volatile family life, and I think Fr. Passeno was concerned about them and wanted Tom to be exposed to healthy activities and a family environment. Fr. Passeno had a good influence on Tom and inspired him to be more religious.

My father worked on the home farm with his four brothers after graduating from Michigan State University and became a "custom-farmer" who contracted with individual downstate to grow apples, cherries, and peach-

es to be sold to markets before later owning his own farm. Tom spent time with our family and would occasionally join us for a meal. I lived on Third Street in the slab town district of Traverse City and Paul Steffes a mutual friend lived just down the alley from me on Second Street Tom lived a few blocks away on Elmwood Street, just down from Immaculate Conception Church. We all lived in pretty close proximity to each other and the Grand Traverse Bay, where we would fish off the Hannah Lay Pier, which was adjacent to the Morgan-McCool cherry and apple canning plant.

Tom also worked at the Conaway's Bowling Alley on Park Street near Front Street and got me a job there too. We would work from 6:30 p.m. until sometimes 10:00 or 11:00 at night, five days a week, setting bowling pins, and got pretty good at it. When it was league night we would have to do two lanes at a time as we hopped over back and forth setting pins, constantly making sure we were in the right lane.

Tom was always a very industrious type of person who maintained a heck of a work ethic and had goals. When we would play ping-pong at my house Tom used the chalkboard that we tallied our scores on to practice his signature. He had two styles, fancy and non-fancy. The fancy style was one that he said he was going to use someday when he was successful.

We lost contact after Tom left Traverse City, but I saw him at several of the reunions. I think starting up Domino's was the highlight of his ambitions because he was able to put all that hard work and planning into creating a business that was so rewarding for him, and he was able to do something that he really loved.

During high school Tom lived on the Crouch farm just south of town on the Boardman River. The long Michigan winters were very cold, and in this particular home you could often see frost and in some places even light coming through the cracks in their walls. There was no electricity, so the family cooked with a wood-burning stove, and they read with a kerosene lamp in the kitchen. Tom would spend hours in the warmth of that kitchen as he indulged himself in some materialistic daydreaming while pouring over Montgomery Ward's or Sears catalogs as he became educated about the quality and cost of the products that filled their pages. In his imagination he would build a home and then fill it with items from those catalogs as he began to visualize what it would be like to have the very best. Those mental construction projects eventually led him to a more detailed knowledge of architecture and to the Traverse City library, where he began to read books about Frank Lloyd Wright. This love for Wright and architecture would become a lifelong dream.

At the Crouches he was able to attend school in Traverse City once again and went to St. Francis High School, where he reconnected with many of his old friends. Tom did well at St. Francis, getting good grades and, while he loved basketball, football and baseball, he couldn't go out for sports because he had to do chores back on the farm. He worked hard for Mr. Crouch, cutting wood and the other odd jobs, and he felt Mr. Crouch must have thought so too because he gave him $2.00 a week for his efforts. Looking back now he can see that his stay there probably also helped supplement the Crouches income because of the difficulty they had in farming their rocky land.

During those years at St. Francis Tom remembers feeling embarrassed by his worn clothes and the holes in his socks and on the soles of his shoes. There were times when he had to scrape the manure off the bottom of his shoes as he went into school and keep his feet on the floor so another student couldn't see the bottom of them. In those days those who had "means" went to the public school, and it was the farmers and the poorer families who sent their kids to the Catholic schools, but Tom felt he was even poorer than most of them. He said he was always conscious of what other kids had. Although he was girl crazy during those high school years, he felt that girls were unavailable to him because of his circumstances.

One day in high school religion class, Sr. Andrea asked, "How do you get to heaven?" The hands of all the smart girls in class hands went up right away as they answered with responses like—lead a good life, love God, and practice the virtues of faith, hope and love but they were all wrong. Tom said he couldn't believe it, he knew the answer. "How do you get there?" He answered, "Die in the state of sanctifying grace." This was a lesson that he had learned well at St. Joe's and one that continued to be reinforced during his life. Because the family he stayed with on the Boardman River were not Catholics Tom arranged to get a ride with a neighbor to Sunday Mass. Even as a boy he saw the importance of Mass and never missed.

MARGARET GALLAGHER SOPHIEA-BUFKA: CLASSMATE OF TOM MONAGHAN'S

I met Tom Monaghan in the ninth grade when we attended St. Francis High School because Immaculate Conception only went up to the eighth grade, and many of those students transferred over for high school. I remember Tom as a sort of scrawny kid who was pretty shy and kept to himself. He was a thinker. Tom told me later that he was always embarrassed by his living situation because his socks didn't match or his shoes had holes in them, but most of us were farmers' children and picked cherries to pay for our school clothes. The wealthier families sent their children to public schools, and those who had less went to the Catholic schools.

Our class was one of the biggest to attend St. Francis at that time. Sr. Roberta was the principal who was considered pretty tough and taught English and literature. She always gave us something to think about. Some of the other sisters were—Sr. Dorothea, who taught typing and shorthand, Sr. Robert Marie, who taught history, and Sr. Andrea, who was our homeroom teacher and favorite who taught biology, chemistry, and Latin. Sr. Andrea was tough on the outside but had a heart of gold, and, we all wanted to take her classes. Years later she told us that she continued to pray for us all every day.

As the years went by and Tom's life became public, I followed his many accomplishments. Whenever we had class reunions Tom came and was still the quiet, unassuming person he has always been. I became more involved when Tom asked if I would help Ken Kleinrichert start the Ave Maria Founders Club in Northern Michigan. It is very easy to be enthused about his latest accomplishment, Ave Maria University. Other classmates of Tom's, Phyllis Taylor (Gertz) and Catherine Birdsey (Plamondon), have also been generous in helping with the Founders Club.

In 2008 I was proud to nominate Tom for the honor of being one of the earliest members of the Hall of Fame for the Grand Traverse Area Catholic Schools. His pictures, along with a few of his accomplishments, are located in a place of honor at St. Francis High School, the school we all attended so many years ago.

(Pictured in the seventh grade photograph at Immaculate Conception School on page 59, Eleanor Jakubeck (Kraft), Carolyn Bristol (Michal), Barbara Flees (King), Dorothy Lewis (Fehrenbach), Kay Mc Ginley (St. Pierre), Barbara Depka (Kratky), Alan Gray, Alice Ann Schopieray (Nelson), Lois Eagleton, Dick Zielinski, Louie Houlihan, Eugene Strang, Tom, and our favorite priest, Rev. Msgr. Russell Passeno.)

One day in the spring of Tom's freshman year in high school, while he was doing chores after school and up to his ankles in shoveling manure, it suddenly occurred to him that his life wasn't going the way he had planned it. Since the second grade he had always intended on being a priest and he couldn't understand how he got so far off track. He decided right then and there that he was going into the seminary and would give up the pursuit of girls, *since he wasn't getting anywhere with them anyway*! When Tom told Fr. Passeno, he was delighted and encouraged him to fill out the application. One of questions asked was "Why do you want to be a priest?" to which Tom easily answered, "To seek the salvation of souls."

His mother paid $250 for his tuition, room, and board and since she was already paying the Crouches $7 per week or $364 a year, this was a savings to her. She did, however, have to buy some clothes. Everything had to be plain and preferably black. Black pants, coats, sweaters, shoes and ties with some white shirts. Tom was then sent to St. Joseph Seminary in Grand Rapids, a diocesan seminary that was two and a half hours from Traverse City. During this time he can remember attending a funeral in the family and receiving a lot of respect and attention as a seminarian. They seemed proud of his decision and he was too.

All the boys at the seminary got homesick except for Tom. He said he was right at home in institutional life with about half of the boys leaving after only a week. The boys were virtually all "A" students in grade school, and Tom held his own, getting a 100 in the first marking period in religion. Greek was another story—he struggled with it. He tended to be a little mischievous, getting into pillow fights in the dorm, and talking during study hall, but nothing too serious, just falling back into the same boy stuff that Tom occasionally did in the orphanage. One day the rector, Monsignor Falicki, called him into his office. Tom had a lot of respect for the man because he had the option to be a catcher with a New York Yankees farm team before he was ordained. Monsignor had a letter in his hand from Tom's mother, who was complaining that he didn't write to her often enough, since he was probably writing more to his Aunt Peg than to his mother at the time. Monsignor Falicki gave him a good chewing out.

A few days later Tom was called in again, but this time he was asked to leave the seminary and told that when he packed his bags to go home for Easter, to pack them for good. He couldn't believe it, he was being kicked out and told that he didn't have a vocation! For all the mischievousness he did, he still felt he was one of the most serious boys there— at least he knew why he wanted to be a priest. He lasted less than a year and was crushed, and when he did return to finish out the tenth grade at St. Francis his heart was no longer in it.

After returning to Traverse City he floundered. Living once again with his mother, the problems continued to escalate, and they would argue often about going out for basketball, as well as the 1948 Nash that she bought with the money from his father's insurance policy. As a normal 16-year-old boy he wanted to drive the car and would borrow it every chance he could, something that caused even more tension between them. One day as he was walking home from basketball practice a police officer pulled up to the curb and asked him if he was Tom Monaghan. When he said yes, the officer flashed his badge at him and told him he was taking him to a home for juvenile delinquents, his mother had signed the order. He said he felt like a criminal but had done nothing wrong. The detention home was located on E. Front and Barlow St. and run by a policeman and his wife, Mr. and Mrs. John Mc Closkey. There were about a dozen kids living in the home, and while Tom was now 17 and older than the others, he was shocked to know that kids could be that bad. The McCloskeys treated him well, however, knowing that he was different.

He continued to attend school each day, but was embarrassed about his situation and would walk a circuitous route back to the detention home so the other kids wouldn't catch on. Only a few of his closest friends and the basketball coach had a clue as to what had happened. After six months his Aunt Peg and Uncle Dan (Mahler), after hearing of his circumstances, petitioned the courts for him to move to Ann Arbor to live with them, and now for the first time since his dad died, Tom felt he was finally living a normal life again.

There were forty-five students in the 1955 graduating class from St. Francis High School, and it was run on the backs of the sisters who devoted their lives to Catholic education, which was something that many learned to appreciate only as they grew older. At Tom's thirtieth St. Francis class reunion, Alan Gray, the boy with whom he played those endless games of ping-pong, gave him a piece of the chalkboard that his father had salvaged from the former Mc Kinley School on Old Mission peninsula, the same one that they used to keep a running tally of their games together as boys. It was signed by his classmates. Even though Tom didn't graduate from St. Francis High School, he would always feel a special connection with that school and the town of Traverse City.

He finished out his senior year at St. Thomas the Apostle High School in Ann Arbor, almost flunking out, but didn't care. One day when he saw his Aunt Peg preparing to send out graduation announcements, it hit him that she didn't know how poorly he was doing in school, so he panicked, not wanting to disappoint her. He went to the pastor, Monsignor Peek, to ask him if there was anything that he could do to graduate with his peers; he sent him to Sr. Rose Di Lourdes, his homeroom teacher. She said that he was a little late to start worrying about this now. When he started to cry she told him, "Alright, I'll let you graduate. You got good grades in the seminary, but don't ever ask me for a college recommendation." So Tom graduated at the bottom of his class with a caption in the Shamrock yearbook reading, *"The harder I try to be good, the worse I get, but I may do something sensational yet!"*

CHAPTER TWO

The Lord's Pizza

"It is written: 'One does not live by bread alone, but by every word that comes forth from the mouth of God.'"
MATTHEW 4:4

After graduation Tom worked various jobs, but he felt wasn't getting anywhere and knew his grades were not good enough for college. He wanted to go into architecture, so he applied to the trade school at Ferris Institute (later becoming Ferris University) in Big Rapids, Michigan for the winter semester of '56, hoping to be a draftsman first and maybe later apply to the college. He was shocked to learn that when he was turned down it was not for academic reasons but because the program was full, so he then applied to the college instead and was accepted!

The cost of college was more than Tom could handle and although he had some money saved, an unexpected dental bill depleted what little he had. Dr. Wally Nieman was just out of dental school and someone Tom found in the Ann Arbor yellow pages. He advised Tom that he needed a root canal and some other dental work, which would cost $250 of the $500 he had saved for school. He knew it was going to be a struggle, but Tom decided to do it anyway, even though it often meant going without food to pay for the books and tuition. Wally ended up becoming a lifelong friend of Tom's and is a devout Catholic.

That summer Tom decided that he would work hard to save enough to make it through the next year, but many of the jobs in the Detroit area didn't pay enough, so he decided to hitchhike to Chicago to try his luck there. As the days of summer were quickly passing by he walked by a post office in Harvey, Illinois, where he saw a recruiter who he thought was with the Army sitting at his desk. He remembered hearing that if you joined the Army you would get your college paid for, so he went in and signed up. He was only 19 at the time.

During the recruiting process he kept hearing the word Marines mentioned, but just assumed that all the military branches were represented there. Then as he filled out the final paperwork, he saw at the bottom of the pages the Marine globe and anchor symbol, so he asked the recruiter, "Is this the army or the Marines?" To which he replied, "The Marines of course" looking at Tom as if he were crazy. By this time Tom had to ask himself, "What's the difference?" So he signed the form just as the sergeant hollered, "Raise your right hand and face the flag." Immediately he found out that the two years of college were out the window. Like many of the recruits, he applied for a desk job, but got infantry instead, which he said was the best thing that could have ever happened to him. He accepted his circumstances and decided to make the best of it.

One day a new recruit showed up in his platoon. He was one of those guys that probably wasn't progressing well and was held back so he ended up with Tom's platoon instead. His name was Oswald and he was from Texas. He was a little guy, quiet and little strange. He lined up next to Tom in their formations and they shared the same eight-man tent. Years later Tom saw his picture on television after the shooting of JFK and shouted "Hey, I know that guy. That's Oswald from Texas!" He said he spent quite a bit of time with him in training but couldn't really say much else about him because Oswald was quiet and he wasn't with them the entire sixteen weeks of boot camp.

While in Okinawa Tom decided that he needed to improve himself not just physically but also mentally and he began a self-improvement program. He read just about every book in the base library, but he especially liked inspirational books and practical books on farming and things that he thought might be helpful to him someday. Although his status in life was still pretty meager, the dreams he had from boyhood were now starting to take a more serious tone. He began to build empires in his head and then visualize the situations and problems that might arise and strategically solve them. He also allowed himself to imagine what it might be like to be successful and wealthy.

It was also during this time, while aboard a ship in the middle of the South Pacific, that Tom laid out what he would call his "five priorities," which became his road map for life. The priorities were spiritual, social, mental, physical, and financial. **Spiritual**: *to be a good Catholic and have a strong relationship with God;* **Social**: *to live by the golden rule;* **Mental**: *to continue to educate himself;* **Physical**: *to care for the body which is the temple of the Holy Spirit;* and **Financial**: *to work hard and save his earnings for future goals.* Tom was always ambitious, so he wanted to make sure he could find a way to include the financial goal, and he was able to do that by concluding that money in its proper place could do a lot of good.

While in the Marines Tom remembers one Sunday, after indulging in a few beers the night before, skipping Mass. The chapel was a half mile walk from the barracks and because he had no ride, he decided to skip. Missing Mass just that one time made it easier to miss the next and before he knew it he had missed almost a dozen times. Shortly after this incident he saw a book about agnostics in the base library that literally scared the "hell" out of him. Through this experience he learned that your faith is never something you can take for granted because, as Yogi Berra once said, "If you don't know where you're going, you might end up someplace else." Tom was taught by the sisters that you were going to spend your eternity either in Heaven or hell, depending on how you lived your life and he never wanted to end up "someplace else." After reading that book he never missed Mass again. It was also during this time that he reconsidered the priesthood once again. He spoke to the military chaplain about possibly becoming an order priest instead of a diocesan one, but when he found out the amount of schooling it involved he finally dismissed the idea of the priesthood once and for all.

He was due to get out of the Marines on July 2, 1959 and couldn't wait. During his time in the Marines he had been saving half of his checks to begin a new life after he was discharged and had about $2,000 saved up, which was a lot in 1959. One day while hitchhiking back to the base he met a slick oil man who made him an offer too good to be true, and he ended up losing everything. He was only 22 years old.

While Tom was in the Marines his mother had remarried and moved back to Ann Arbor; so had his brother Jim. Jim lived in a small attic apartment and invited Tom to move in with him as well as giving him a rusted out '49 Plymouth, which he was grateful for. He got a job in charge of the paper boys at the *Washtenaw News* and scraped together enough money for tuition at the University of Michigan, but he had no money for books, so after three weeks he dropped out, hoping to try again the next semester.

He started a Sunday *New York Times* home delivery route and bought a newsstand for $500. To sell subscriptions he would knock on doors in the wealthier sections of Ann Arbor and eventually had 185 customers, who he delivered to from his car, which took him almost four hours. This simple venture, he said, taught him a lot about offering customers a unique service, and also about home delivery. It also taught him that when you see an opportunity, it is important to seize it, which was a lesson that greatly benefited him later.

When he did return to school the second semester he was working so many hours that there was no time to study, so he had to drop out again. At 23 he was still a freshman in college, driving a beat-up car, and not getting anywhere financially, but even more importantly he felt that any dreams he had for the future were falling apart. It was around this same time that his brother Jim approached him about buying a pizza place in Ypsilanti near Eastern Michigan University. Jim was a mailman and would stop in for lunch at a place called DomiNick's, and the owner was interested in selling. The idea that began to form was that they would each work a shift, and since most pizzerias were open only at night, this would give Tom plenty of time and income to return to college. He only had $77 in the bank at the time, but they borrowed $500 from a local credit union, as well as assuming the loans for the equipment, and plunged in. Tom got pretty excited about the prospect of not only becoming a great architect but now also an entrepreneur! They wanted to call the pizzeria Monaghan's Italian Pizza but they didn't have enough money to change the sign, so they talked to Dominic DiVarti, who agreed to let them keep the name and the sign!

They opened the doors to DomiNick's on December 9, 1960 because Tom didn't want to miss Mass on December 8th a Holy Day of the Catholic Church and the Feast Day of the Immaculate Conception. He also struggled with being open on Sundays because it was the busiest day of the week since the Eastern Michigan University cafeteria was closed and the majority of their business came from the dorms, but he talked with a priest who told him it was okay. Right after they signed the papers, Jim stopped by to tell him that he wanted out of the business. He was getting cold feet about leaving the security of his job at the post office, so from that point on Tom had no other choice but to run the business full time by himself. This eliminated any idea he had of going back to college. At first he was disappointed, but then decided that if he was going to be in the pizza business, it was going to be the best in the country!

Dominick gave him a fifteen-minute lesson on making pizzas and Tom said he will never forget his first order. The customer came in and ordered a pizza at the front counter, and what a sense of relief Tom felt when he said he'd be back to pick it up. He had no idea what he was doing, but that would be the first of millions of pizzas that he would sell. In that first week they made about $99, but soon he was working almost every waking hour of the day and losing money every week. He had rented a room across the street, and the bills were piling up, so he couldn't afford the $49 a month payment on the '55 Ford wagon he bought for his newspaper business. Most of the meals he ate were pizzas, and those were usually bad orders or burnt ones, but occasionally he would buy goods from the bakery next door that were too old to sell at full price. In the beginning they couldn't even afford a phone, which is pretty amazing to think of—a pizza business without a phone!

Tom had a lot to learn. He would prepare all day for the rushes at night, but one evening when they were ready to open the doors half the staff didn't show up. He made the decision to limit the sizes and type of pizza they made, and it turned out to be their most profitable night ever. Keeping the menu simple turned out to be a winning formula for Domino's for many years. Now he was able to pay his bills and make some money. He was finally a success—well sort of.

After the Ypsilanti store became profitable, he began looking for other locations and settled on Central Michigan University in Mount Pleasant. CMU had at least four times as many dorms as Eastern Michigan University since Eastern was more of a commuter college due to its proximity to Detroit. He financed $2200 worth of used equipment, signed the $60 a month lease, and called the new store, "Pizza King." After signing that agreement to open the new store, he laid in bed that night, scared to death and wondering, "Why am I taking a risk on that second store when the first one is doing so well?" But the lease was signed and the equipment purchased, so he was committed. In the 1980s he was given the award for Entrepreneur of the Decade, which he said was pretty funny considering how scared he was to open that second store. It was a real leap in faith.

NORINE LOZON: TOM MONAGHAN'S COUSIN

In the early 1990s we had a family reunion at the homestead in Ann Arbor. I was deciding whether or not to purchase a small apartment building in Plymouth, Michigan. The down payment on the four-unit building would have taken all of my savings at the time, and I didn't know if I would have been able to lease out the units and make a profit, so I was hesitant to make the deal - afraid of failing. I had a conversation with Tom about taking risks.

I asked Tom how he was able to overcome his fear of failure. He said that he took a lot of risks to get where he was today, and it was just a way of life for him. He knew that in the worst-case scenario, if he lost every-thing, he could always go back to flipping pizzas and make a living that way. And if he lost everything, he still had God and his faith, which was more important than his possessions.

Tom really minimalized the consequences of risk for me when he put into perspective the value of material goods. So really, if I lost everything on that real estate deal, I really wouldn't be that bad off, because look at what I would have left—God's love and grace.

I forged ahead and bought that small apartment building, and it did end up going well for me. That was twenty years ago. I now realize that wealth is temporary, because it's of this earth and real riches are stored up in Heaven and evidenced by faith in action.

During the first few months Tom was busy training people to make pizzas and work other jobs in the new store. His full-time man was Frank Sukovitch, and Frank was getting pretty good at making pizzas and learning how to run things. Business was pretty slow at the early part of one particular evening, so at the spur of the moment Tom asked Frank to take over so he could make a delivery, just to get out of the store. This was February 1961, only fourteen months after he got into the pizza business.

He took a delivery to Sweeny Hall, a girls' dorm at CMU. In those days the switchboard operator would call the room and the customer would come down and pick up her pizza. Tom was pretty taken by the girl at the switchboard. Being pretty shy with girls, he tried to strike up a conversation with her, but it didn't get very far because the customer came down to get her pizza, so he headed back to the store. As he was driving back he was still on cloud nine, thinking the switchboard girl was as cute as a "bug's ear," so by the time he arrived at the store he had made the decision to call her and ask her out for a date. It took several attempts as he worked his way through a maze of dead ends trying to find out who was at the desk that evening, but eventually he found out her name was Margie Zybach, and when he asked her out, she said yes!

He told Margie that he was going to be a millionaire by the age of thirty, to which she chuckled, saying, "That's a good line." But Tom was dead serious. There was absolutely no doubt in his mind that he wouldn't attain his dream. By their second date he was hooked and decided he was going to propose, but because she had only known him for such a short time, he had to convince her that he was serious. Tom had a dental appointment with his friend Wally Nieman in Ann Arbor, and remembered a jewelry store across the street from where he had his newsstand. The owner, Moray, used to buy a paper from Tom every day so Tom thought maybe he knew him well enough to ask him for an engagement ring with no money down. Moray was very accommodating and even agreed to take the ring back if the answer was no.

On Tom's third date with Margie, he popped the question. Margie took the ring and said she would have to think about it, but within a week she agreed and they set the date for August 25, 1962. Margie and Tom were married by Fr. Patrick Jackson at St. Thomas the Apostle Church in Ann Arbor. This was the same church that his parents were married in on April 14, 1936, and whose outer walls contain many of the field stones obtained from the family farm that his father tended to. This was the church that Tom and his family went to as a young boy, and one that his own family would also be part of in the coming years. Both Jim and his mother attended the wedding. Through the years Tom's relationship with his mother had changed quite a bit from the one he had when he was young. He saw her as a good woman who really cared for her boys and wanted to do the right thing. Tom's mother died at the age of 73 and remained a good Catholic her entire life.

WALTER NIEMAN: FRIEND AND DENTIST IN ANN ARBOR, MI

I met Tom Monaghan in 1955, and needless to say, over the years I have had fun relating stories about Tom and his family. One of his endeavors was to have the first New York Times *route west of the Alleghenies. Having a large family, things were kind of tough in those days. Tom made arrangements for me to receive the* New York Times—*as a way of paying off his dental bill. People often say to me, "Is that why you remember Tom Monaghan?" And I tell them, "No, I remember him because my wife wanted the dollar and not the paper!"*

My office staff and I were pleased to be included in a very special occasion in Tom's life. Unexpectedly one early afternoon, he stopped by my office to show us something. He opened a small box, showing us a diamond ring, and said he was on his way up to Mount Pleasant to visit and propose to his girlfriend, Margie. I had not met her before, but I surmised she was going to be very happy considering how Tom was acting. Years later, as Tom's family grew, my staff would help Margie give the babies their bottles as they waited in my reception room.

On another occasion I visited their home off I-94 and Carpenter Road on Ruby Street, and Margie was working on the Domino's Pizza records because, as you know, she did a lot of the bookwork. I was surprised to see that all her records were being kept in a shoe box. That is amazing when you think about it, that years later when they had over fourteen hundred stores that it all started in a shoe box!

I used to travel with Tom to different shops or stores, taking pictures of the night signs and operations because we were working up a slideshow to help promote Domino's as a franchise. When you thought of hamburgers you associated with McDonald's; when you thought of chicken, Kentucky Fried so the promotional idea was to mention pizza and think of Domino's, especially since they were the only home delivery stores. I am sure the early days were very stressful for Tom and the girls. The pizza business was a late afternoon and practically all-night business. The managers worked into the wee hours after closing, until about two o'clock in the morning. It was tough on family life.

Tom was always an avid baseball fan. One time when the Tigers had clinched the pennant, which I think it was in St. Louis, they were scheduled to arrive back in Detroit in the late afternoon at Metro Airport. Tom had the idea to go to the airport with a truckload of pizzas and some close friends, of which I was included. We gathered at the original pizza store in Ypsilanti on Cross Street, five or six of us plus a load of pizzas, and headed out I-94 to Detroit Metro Airport. Much to our surprise, when we were about four blocks off the interstate entrance to the airport, we came to a dead stop as it seemed a lot of the fans had the same idea as we did. After sitting around for 15 or 20 minutes, we tried the radio and found out the Tigers were now going to land at Willow Run Airport. What a disappointment! So we ended up eating, selling, and giving away pizzas to the other stranded Tiger fans instead. It was quite late before we got home that night, and never did see the Tigers.

Tom was always an honest and loyal person. I remember when he was having financial troubles with Domino's after being away from it for a awhile, he told his suppliers, "Stick with me and I will get it going again." Most of them did support him, and he ended up making millionaires out of all of them.

In a few short years Tom's pizza business had grown to three stores, and he was probably doing the highest volume in Michigan due to their locations around college campuses and because of their fast delivery. It was around this time that Dominick DiVarti called to say they couldn't use his name anymore. "Why not?" Tom asked, to which Dominick replied, "My customers are getting confused." So accepting his situation, he enlisted his employees in the search for a new name.

One day in 1965, Jim Kennedy, one of Tom's top employees, came back from a delivery at a shoe store and shouted, "I've got our new name! Domino's!" which Tom replied, "That's it! Where did you get it?" Jim said that when he walked in the store the salesman shouted, "Hey, there's the guy from Domino's!"—just like that history was made. Immediately, in his enthusiasm, Tom thought of the domino and said, "We'll put three dots on it, one for each store." At that time they had two pizzerias in Ypsilanti and one in Ann Arbor, but thought later what that domino would've looked like with 11,000 dots on it! *Years later Tom also found out that the word "Dominus" in Latin means "Lord" so really, right from the beginning, Domino's was the "Lord's Pizza."*

During the coming years many innovations were created by Domino's that became the standard in the pizza industry. From corrugated boxes to heated pouches, conveyer ovens to dough trays and commissaries, everything worked together to create an excellent product and to shorten the time for delivery because delivery, was the key to success!

CHAPTER THREE

The Sin of Pride

"Again I tell you, it is easier for a camel to go through the eye of a needle than for a rich man to enter the kingdom of God."
MATTHEW 19:24

As the pizza business grew, Tom's family grew too. His first daughter was named Mary, followed by Susie, Margaret (Maggie), and Barbara, four girls in all, and he was delighted. They all grew up with Domino's as part of an extended family. Margie was also a very integral part of the business, doing the book keeping for many years and pitching in at the store wherever she was needed. Tom worked many long hours but saw it as a labor of love. During the early years of their marriage, Tom attended Mass Sundays and went to confession several times a year, but not much else. On Sunday's he often arrived late just before the offertory.

They sent the girls to Catholic schools, and although they were on a meager income Tom was willing to make the sacrifice, thinking they would get the good formation that he had as a boy. What he found out too late was the schools were actually teaching them very little about their faith and, in some cases, undermining it, which made him realize they probably would've been better off in a public school and taught their faith at home instead.

As Domino's continued to grow, their need for space also grew, causing them to move the headquarters four times over an eight-year period. In 1984 Tom purchased a 300-acre plot of farmland in one of the best locations in Ann Arbor and started what would become known as "Domino's Farms." The notion of having his headquarters on a farm was something he had thought about for a long time, and it was here he was finally able to merge his love for architecture and those fond memories of his life on a farm. As Domino's Farms was being built, Tom also included a small Catholic chapel for the benefit of the employees. Currently, the chapel offers four masses a day, Monday to Friday, and many opportunities for confession. It is available to both Catholics and non-Catholics alike to stop by to meditate and pray.

In the fall of 1983, as Domino's was financially doing well and Tom no longer had to pinch pennies, he began to enjoy some of the things he had always dreamed of. One of the big turning points in his life was the purchase of the Detroit Tigers. He had always been a big Tigers fan, starting with their World Series win in 1945 at the age of seven. In the orphanage the boys were all Tigers fans. Tom never even heard of the Detroit Lions until he was about eleven or twelve. The Pistons were in Fort Wayne, and the Red Wings existed, but since the boys in the orphanage didn't skate there was little interest in them. So it was all Tigers, and baseball was indeed the national pastime!

The highlight of the year in the orphanage was their annual trip to Briggs stadium with the Knights of Columbus to see the Tigers game. Their heroes were Hal Neuhauser, Hank Greenburg, George Kell, Fred Hutchinson, Dizzy Trout, Virgil Trucks, and Hoot Evers. They would be glued to the radio and couldn't wait for baseball season to start, each having their own favorite player, and for Tom it was Hoot Evers and his number 14. Harry Hellman was the radio announcer who, in Tom's opinion, was the best ever and since there was no television, radio was their only link to the Tigers.

He had always hoped someday to be able to purchase the Tigers, and since Mr. John Fetzer, the owner, was in his eighties, there was now speculation that he might be selling. There were a lot of prominent Michigan names being mentioned, because at that time baseball had a rule that all owners had to be local, but Domino's was not even on the radar because they were not that well known in the Detroit area. By this time their stores were scattered all over the country, mostly in college towns and near military bases.

Tom found his justification for purchasing the Tigers by attending one of the YPO (Young Presidents Organization) meetings, where Fred Wilpon, the owner of the New York Mets, spoke and told how the purchase of the Mets helped his business grow.

That spring he and his daughter Maggie visited Jim Campbell, the president, at the Tigers' spring training camp in Lakeland, Florida, hoping to make his pitch. Whatever he said apparently worked, because Mr. Fetzer called asking that he meet with him at his hotel. From Tom's perspective the meeting didn't start out well as Tom listened to Fetzer's long discourse on baseball. After what seemed to be an endless dissertation Fetzer finally asked Tom to tell him something about himself. Tom shared with him some things about his childhood, about his dad's death when Tom was four, living in the orphanage, and his lifelong love for baseball, as well as the history of his business career. As it turns out they had very similar backgrounds. Fetzer shared his own stories about losing his dad at a young age and his own experience of growing up a Tigers fan. Fetzer was a pioneer in the radio business and so, like Tom, they both found their success in delivery. Soon after his return to Michigan, Mr. Fetzer's office called Tom again to set up another meeting, and before long Tom's boyhood dream of becoming part of the Tigers had become a reality!

Sparky Anderson, the legendary manager for the Tigers, predicted that they would win the pennant within five years of him taking the job, and since Tom purchased the team in Sparky's fourth year with the Tigers, this proved to be a real asset for him. The new ownership of the Tigers boosted the morale in Domino's, and winning the 1984 World Series gave the company the national recognition it was looking for.

The first time Tom met Sparky, he told him about his boyhood dream

playing shortstop for the team, to which Sparky replied, "I
her too, but she ain't gonna pitch for me!" Tom organized
ions with the boys from the orphanage to see the Tigers
again. The same boys he used to huddle around the radio with as a
young boy. He believed that Sr. Beranda would've been very happy to
see them there together, and for Tom her prophetic words were now
coming true. "Well, I don't think that's ever been done before, Tommy, but if you want to do it there's no reason you can't." For years Tom
Monaghan had struggled and pursued success, and now his life had
become the classic Horatio Alger story, going from "rags to riches," but
with so much publicity and wealth he started to get carried away.

Using the same justification that he did when he purchased the Tigers, Tom began purchasing many other luxuries, from jets, to yachts,
to cars. When he purchased the 1929 Duisenberg that won the Triple
Crown, for $1 million at the Harrah's auction, he said he actually want-
ed the price to go up so it would be the most expensive classic car ever
purchased, to generate publicity and give the company exposure. Some
referred to this as "conspicuous consumption." Maybe if he had stopped
there it would have been alright, but he found it adrenaline-building
and soon his desire for the best of everything had him moving at a diz-
zying pace. He was walking a tight rope during the 80's, trying to enjoy
everything that this world offered and be a good Catholic at the same
time. He realized at one point what he wanted to be was a "billionaire
saint," to have everything in this world and the next.

Tom had been doing a lot of spiritual reading, and Dinesh D' Souza
was one of his favorite authors. In one of his books he included a list of
other books that Catholics should read, such as *Seven Story Mountain*
by Thomas Merton and *Orthodoxy* by G.K. Chesterton. Tom read every
book on the list, but the one that would change his life was *Mere Christianity* by C. S. Lewis. In there was a chapter called, "The Great Sin" and
it was about *pride*. Tom was always taught that pride was the greatest
of all sins, and the source of all sins but in that chapter he learned that
the reason he wanted all those luxuries was not for their convenience or
their beauty but solely to impress people. He knew that he always had

the problem of wanting to impress people. This most likely stemmed from being brought up so poor, but he felt he was a special case. He said he had two phases: the first was to get to the point of not being embarrassed and fit in, but the next millisecond he was dissatisfied with that state and wanted to stand out above the others. Lewis wrote, "We say that people are proud of being rich, or clever, or good looking, but they are not. They are proud of being richer, or cleverer, or better looking than others. It is the comparison that makes you proud: *the pleasure of being above the rest.*" After reading C. S. Lewis he realized that those things that he thought were good, such as being competitive, driving for success, and always trying harder than anybody else weren't necessarily that good after all if they were done for the wrong reason. He had worked hard so he could someday have the best, but now he had to ask himself, why? Was it because he wanted to be better than others? This was a sobering dose of reality for Tom. He always saw himself as someone who, when success came, would be able to handle it because, after all, he was a good Catholic. He had his five priorities, so he knew what was important, but with *Mere Christianity* Lewis had hit a central truth that he needed to consider. He needed to face up to the sin of pride and do something about it!

From that moment on Tom took what he called the "Millionaire Vow of Poverty." He decided to give up all ostentatious luxuries, not conveniences, but show off luxuries. There was no more interest in driving Ferraris or Rolls Royces. He sold the jets and yachts as well as many of his other collections, realizing that he had used excuses like "time is money" or "they were good exposure for the business" while knowing deep inside the truth. This vow began to change his life, and before long he found himself more content and at peace. The late Chuck Colson, who was the former White House special counsel and head of Prison Fellowship, said that it was this very chapter in Lewis's book that changed the course of his life too. Pride is something Tom said he will most likely have to fight his entire life, but he was willing to work at it and start living his life for God. He equated it to someone who had stopped using drugs; it was a relief.

It was around this same time that Tom also met a "Lady" who, along with C. S. Lewis, saved him from this "train wreck." He was on a vacation with his family in Europe and decided to visit the small village of Medjugorie, which was then part of the Socialist country of Yugoslavia and where the Blessed Mother had been allegedly appearing to six children since June of 1981. He was excited to know that something like this was happening in his lifetime and felt the need to check it out. Tom and his daughter were invited into St. James Rectory during the time of one of the apparitions, and although he finds it difficult to describe, he has no doubts that the Blessed Mother was there. Since that time he has had a relationship with her that is hard to put into words. He knows that she is real, close, and someone who he can always talk with. After building Ave Maria, he was asked at a public event, "Why do you always name everything Ave Maria? Why is Mary so important to you?" He thought about it for a short time and then said, quietly: "I don't know, I guess she is my friend."

In Medjugorie Our Lady asked for three things, Mass, confession, and the rosary, so Tom began to increase his rosaries because this was not just something she asked for at Medjugorie but during her past appearances at Fatima and Lourdes too. He heard that Don Shula, who had a perfect season with the Miami Dolphins in1972, attended daily Mass, which impressed him. He figured if Don Shula with his busy schedule, could make time for daily Mass, then what was his excuse? Someone asked Mother Teresa once where she got her energy to do the work she did in serving the poor, and she said it was the Eucharist. Tom said daily Mass and the Rosary were the best things that he ever did in his life because of their tremendous impact on everything else. Regular confession is important too because through it you receive God's healing and forgiveness. Once these things were put into the proper order in his life, God began to show Tom what real riches were.

RALPH MARTIN: PRESIDENT, RENEWAL MINISTRIES

One day, while attending Mass at St. Thomas the Apostle Church in Ann Arbor, a man tapped me on the shoulder and asked if I was Ralph Martin. I said I was and the man introduced himself as Tom Monaghan and told me he was reading my book, Hungry for God, *and was finding it helpful. We ended up getting together to talk, and that began a relationship that has now spanned decades. Tom was grappling with what it meant to give himself fully to God and the Church, and we had many conversations about that.*

One of the most significant conversations, it turned out, was when Tom said he was planning to give a lot of money to a Catholic institution that I knew was in a state of doctrinal and moral confusion. I pointed that out to him and showed him the evidence. He was shocked that not everything that had the name 'Catholic' attached to it was really Catholic in terms of being faithful to Church teaching. That began his own process of growth and discernment, in which he learned how to distinguish what was sound and what was not so sound in the many appeals for funding that were made to him.

I admire Tom very much for his desire to spend his whole life and resources in the service of Christ and the Church, his humility in admitting his various mistakes, and his determination to persevere to the end as a faithful son of the Church.

CHAPTER FOUR

Catholic Causes

"Go into all the world and preach the good news."
MARK 16:15

As a Catholic Tom was always pro-life; however, he did not get actively involved in any way. In 1989 there was a ballot proposal in Michigan, regarding the issue to stop tax-funded abortions and the polls showed that they were losing. He was asked to help fund a television commercial agreeing to match any money raised up to $50,000, and agreed to participate. He knew he was getting himself into the fray in a public way, but did it anyway. Shortly afterward he started to get calls from franchises complaining that a national boycott was organized against Domino's by the NOW group (National Organization of Women), which could potentially kill their sales. Tom started to feel helpless wondering how he was going to overcome this, when a great calm came over him as he thought, "If the company goes down over this, at least it's for a good reason."

After the dust settled and he did successfully survive the NOW attack, Tom decided he wanted to get more involved in the pro-life movement and other Catholic causes, but did not want to jeopardize Domino's in the future, so he needed to get himself in a position where he and the company would be less vulnerable. He had already started the Thomas S. Monaghan Foundation, which was used for his early philanthropic efforts, but as Domino's grew it later evolved into the Domino's Foundation to disperse funds for a variety of charitable endeavors. When he began to focus more on Catholic causes, the name was changed to the Mater Christi Foundation (Latin for Mother of Christ). Although this was a beautiful title, many had a hard time understanding it, so the name was finally changed to the Ave Maria Foundation, under which it still exists today. Tom felt that the name Ave Maria was something that many people were familiar with because of the Franz Shubert composition and because it was the salutation that the Archangel Gabriel used in greeting Mary at the Annunciation (Ave Maria is Latin for Hail Mary). The Ave Maria Foundation was established as a lay apostolate to focus on a broad range of Catholic projects, from education to the media, as well as community projects and other Catholic charities.

In 1987 one of the firstfruits of this foundation was Legatus (Latin for ambassador). As Tom was approaching his 50th birthday, he was attending his last YPO meeting (Young Presidents Organization). Tom had experienced great fellowship and networking for his business in YPO but was no longer eligible to be a member after the age of 50. That year the convention was being held in Venice, Italy, so he contacted Cardinal Edmund Szoka, who was then the Archbishop of Detroit, to see if the Cardinal could assist him in obtaining an audience with the Holy Father, John Paul II. Tom said he was honored to be able to attend Mass in the Pope's private chapel in the Vatican and receive Holy Communion from him. What impressed him most were his blue eyes looking into his as the Pope placed the Eucharist on his tongue. Afterward Tom was able to meet the Holy Father personally, and he saw that visit as a tremendous privilege for him as a Catholic and a high point of his life.

About an hour after leaving that audience with the Pope, he felt like a lightning bolt had hit him as he began thinking about establishing a Catholic organization that would be similar to the YPO to help support and foster Catholic business leaders in their faith. It made him think that while there were some people who had achieved material wealth and whose focus was not on God, he believed that there were many more individuals who did have a strong devotion to their faith and made it their top priority. They had been tested by the many temptations that money could bring but remained faithful so they could become ambassadors for the Church. Tom saw Legatus as an organization that could provide an environment to support them on their spiritual journey and help them live and spread the teachings of their faith.

Since that time Legatus has grown into a substantial organization that brings Catholic business leaders and their spouses (who are automatic members) together for monthly meetings that include Confession, Rosary, Mass, and a meal with great speakers, held in various parts of the country. Unlike the YPO, there is no age restriction. Legatus currently has approximately 4,800 member,s with nearly 2,500 of them CEOs, and 85 chapters across North America, with 10 percent of the member dues presented to the Holy Father each year.

One year, as they attended an audience with the Holy Father in Rome, John Paul II addressed the members by saying, "The world needs genuine witnesses to the Christian ethics in the field of business, and the Church asks you to fulfill this role publicly and with perseverance." John Paul II was canonized a saint of the Church on April 27, 2014, Divine Mercy Sunday, along with Pope John XXIII. Many refer to him as John Paul the Great, and for Tom, he believes that title describes the Holy Father accurately. When he was in his presence he knew he was in the presence of a saint and a great, great man.

On January 25, 1985 at the Extraordinary Assembly of the Synod of Bishops, which was convened by John Paul II on the 20th anniversary of the close of the Second Vatican Council, the decision was made to publish a new Catechism of the Catholic Church. John Paul II put together a commission of cardinals and bishops to oversee such a monumental project, but due to financial constraints they were unable to move forward. Tom met with Cardinal Ratzinger (who would eventually be Pope Benedict XVI) and Austria's Cardinal Christoph Schonborn to discuss their needs, and Tom agreed to offer the financial support to help fund their costs for research, travel, staff, and the equipment needed to complete the project. The New Catechism was released in October 1992.

Cardinal Schonborn spoke to a group of Legatus members on the Catechism's 20th anniversary and the beginning of the Year of Faith on October 11, 2012, stating that he thanked Tom Monaghan for funding the Catechism and that without his assistance the Catechism may have never been published. Tom saw this as a significant investment on his part because it has been an important tool of revitalizing the Church, as well as being the first Catechism in five hundred years.

By December 1991, as Tom's attention went to other projects and as he stepped away from the day-to-day operation at Domino's, the company began to struggle. To satisfy the banks, the first thing he had to do was get rid of all business that was not an integral part of Domino's, to allow him to focus more on the company and provide some badly needed cash. The big one that had to go was the ownership of the Tigers. This wasn't a good time to be selling; it was now 1992 and the economy was weak.

There were some big Michigan names who were interested in the Tigers in the past, so Tom contacted a few of them, but there was no interest. Al Taubman, Rich DeVos from Amway, and Dick Manoogian had all been interested earlier, but the timing was bad. A group of Legatus members even tried to put a consortium together, but it didn't pan out. He finally hired Goldman Sachs to sell the club but the only buyer with any wherewithal was Mike Ilitch, the owner of Little Caesars, whose two-for-one pizza pricing during those hard economic times was having great success. Edsel Ford was also interested but he was offering only half of the asking price, so the club was sold to Ilitch in July of 1992.

Many of those at Domino's thought it was terrible to sell the team to a competitor, and selling the Tigers was a bitter pill for Tom to swallow. It had always been his hope that the Tigers would be something he could pass on to his own family. Owning the team was the ultimate dream of his childhood and adult life, and no other sports team would ever be a close second. Sometimes he wondered if maybe he should have gutted it out, but he was dealing with the banks and he didn't want to see the team suffer and wait for the company to recover.

By July 1994 the company was on solid footing and growing again, which allowed Tom to continue with some of the charitable projects that he had delayed or curtailed earlier, including building a cathedral in the earthquake and war torn country of Nicaragua, as well as opening schools, supporting an orphanage, and opening a mission in Zacapa, Honduras. During the building of the cathedral in Nicaragua, protests were organized outside Tom's parish church of St. Thomas the Apostle Church in Ann Arbor, as protestors used the mantra "bread not bricks." Tom felt the protests were absurd considering he was giving the people in this extremely poor country jobs to feed their families. He also believed that by building the cathedral they would have bread that would feed their souls. It was through situations like this that Tom grew stronger and learned to follow his own discernment. Over the years Tom never kept his Catholic faith a secret. Consequently he was frequently contacted by many Catholic charities and causes. Over a period of time he narrowed them down to what he considered the most important; Catholic education and the media.

The main media was television. He believed that Mother Angelica did an outstanding job with the Eternal Word Television Network (EWTN) and through it brought more people into the Church and back to their faith than any one person in recent history. He considers her a world class entrepreneur. Her secret to success was summed up in the book, *Mother Angelica's Book of Life Lessons and Everyday Spirituality*, by Raymond Arroyo's where she said, "Once I get an inspiration, I never question it. I know myself and I believe that if God wants it, He has a plan. If you are following God, He never shows you the end. It's always a walk of faith. Franciscan virtue is to follow the Providence of God and God's Providence goes as far as you go. Now that's the scary thing about it. If you don't go, He won't go." To Tom, Mother Angeli
of the stuff that saints are made of, irascible types, tough c
plenty of faults, but with a faith and determination like F

willing to jump out of the boat first and ask questions later.

Mother Angelica was encouraging many to go into radio because she already had the programming, which is a big cost of operating a radio station. There were about 1,600 Protestant radio stations in the U.S. at that time, and Catholics were way behind in this apostolate. Mother offered her television programming to anyone who wanted to use it to start a Catholic radio station, so Tom became the first to take her up on this offer. In 1996 Ave Maria Communications was launched, and Al Kresta was hired as its director. As a former Protestant minister he had once hosted a highly popular Christian radio program in the Detroit area on WMUZ during the 1980s and 90s called, "Talk from the Heart." Al's search for the truth eventually led him back to a reconversion in his own Catholic faith, and to the formation of Ave Maria Radio, which he currently runs today as its CEO and president. Starting with a small rented daytime station in Ann Arbor, it was the first full-time Catholic radio station in the country at that time. Today Ave Maria Radio and EWTN can be heard on more than 250 Catholic radio stations through-out the country, with more being added each month. Catholic radio has certainly filled a niche and has become a great tool of evangelization in this mobile society, as many cradle Catholics are being reeducated in their faith, and through it many non-Catholics are learning the truths of the Catholic Church for the first time. Once Tom felt assured that the media was being covered, he began to look to education.

AL KRESTA: PRESIDENT AND CEO OF AVE MARIA RADIO, AND HOST OF KRESTA IN THE AFTERNOON

After serving as an evangelical Protestant pastor for five years, I realized that I was, at heart, a Catholic and in 1992 returned to the Church in which I had been baptized as an infant. I had known of Tom Monaghan for many years before I met him. He had an admirable reputation and seemed to take his faith quite seriously, so when his assistant, Betsy Kanitz, asked if I would speak at one of Tom's First Friday Breakfasts sometime in the early 1990s, I was eager to meet him. I gave a talk sketching my spiritual journey, which was well received, and Tom was enthusiastic; I was also encouraged. This was one of my first talks as a Catholic.

At that time Tom asked if I was interested in Catholic radio, and I told him it was a good idea, someone ought to try it. I was interested enough to look into it and made some inquiries with Bill Steltemeier at EWTN, and Terry Coles, who was involved in radio in Canada, but there didn't seem to be a passion for the formation of a Catholic radio network or cluster of stations.

In 1996, Sally and I had been praying over a two-year period about where to move our family. Our Detroit neighborhood was deteriorating, and while my wife and I had moved there as missionaries, our kids didn't necessarily have the same spiritual obligations. Around this same time Sally went on pilgrimage to the Holy Land with a group from Christ the King in Ann Arbor led by its pastor, Fr. Ed Fride. Christ the King consisted of an evangelical and charismatic congregation that truly lived as though the faith was the most important concern for a family's life, and we wanted to raise our children in this kind of environment. I had a number of friends and acquaintances there as well, so we started looking into the Ann Arbor/Ypsilanti area.

We wanted a house that would provide extra rooms so we could create an extended family for college students who were interested in integrating their faith with their studies. I had a library of 25,000 books and we wanted to share our faith, family, and academic resources with these young people in transition. We looked at a Buddhist retreat center in Ypsilanti, which had a good layout and enough room, but our bid failed, and by the end of 1996 we were ready to build.

Little did I know that during that same time Tom had responded to a challenge of Mother Angelica of EWTN to lease or buy radio stations. In September of 1996, Tom deputized Frank Czajka to lease a tiny AM signal in Ann Arbor that reached as many cows as it did humans but it was sufficient to put Tom officially into the radio business, and WDEO was born, incorporating the Latin word for God (Deo) in the call letters. It turned out to be the first EWTN affiliate to begin broadcasting Mother

Angelica's programming 24 hours a day.

I got hit with a flu that put me on my back through Christmas and New Years 1996-97, but when I did finally go back to work in January, and before I could reschedule with the realtor, Tom phoned, asking me if I was interested in the job of media manager. His current media manager, Gerry Rauch, was planning on a move, and Tom needed someone to head up his fledgling media apostolate, which at the time consisted of the Credo, a monthly tabloid-size newspaper serving the southeast corner of the Lansing diocese, and WDEO, 1290 AM. I suspect that Fr. Pat Egan, who had recently begun the Ann Arbor Catholic Men's Movement and who was considered the Pizza Priest, or chaplain, for Domino's Farm, told him I was looking for a place to live in Ann Arbor.

We met on a Saturday afternoon, and I immediately remembered why I liked Tom. He had a self-effacing manner that reflected a powerful evidence of humility, and he hadn't been born with a silver spoon in his mouth. We began talking about the year I had lived on the street as he shared some of his own hard times as a teenager. It was clear Tom was searching for a simpler, less materialistic, less driven way of life that would provide greater opportunity for the charitable works he had come to value over the concerns of business and conspicuous consumption. He'd already started Catholic schools, launched an overseas mission, replaced an earthquake-ravaged cathedral in Nicaragua, and founded Legatus, a fraternal organization for Catholic business leaders. Those accomplishments touched his soul far more deeply than overcoming the financial quakes that had shaken Domino's, or fighting a boycott brought by the National Organization for Women because of his support for pro-life causes. He longed to focus his energy and resources on philanthropy fulltime, and had a global vision for Catholic outreach through education. I was also interested in education, but through the media rather than through school systems.

His offer seemed like a tremendously exciting opportunity and nothing less than Heaven-sent, since it would put us in Ann Arbor, but given our vision of ministering to students, the salary offer didn't meet our needs. Then when I laid out our evangelistic plan, he came across with an even better offer. Not only was the salary higher, but he would give us use of a property he owned which included three buildings: a house for my family, a second house for the student residence, and an out-building for a library and study center. This was truly an offer we couldn't refuse.

We moved to Ann Arbor in February of 1997 to serve as missionaries charged with the task of increasing the readership of Credo, *and its frequency from monthly to weekly. We also had the responsibility of developing a Catholic radio station to serve the Ann Arbor area and to figure out a way to syndicate my daily talk program. Over the next two years Credo managed to become a weekly newspaper, and I then turned my attention to radio.*

I set about staffing, installing, and then expanding studio facilities at Domino's Farms, and our first efforts at audience promotion. We acquired a 9,200-watt Christian music station, WWCM, that broadcasted 24 hours a day at 990 on the AM band and WDEO's call letters and programming were migrated over to that frequency. I also launched my new show, called "Kresta in the Morning," and, on a later time shift, "Kresta in the Afternoon," and began developing other features, at first to supplement the material provided by EWTN, but eventually to build a comprehensive schedule of original Catholic radio offerings.

Tom had sold Domino's Pizza in 1998 and was in an organization building whirlwind. All this and more constituted an absolute frenzy of activity that held serious implications for Ave Maria Radio's financial future. From early on, Tom had made clear his expectation that the radio operation would eventually become self-sustaining. As the costs of these other enterprises mounted, the need for fulfilling his expectation became increasingly urgent and since 2002 has been a matter of survival for us. In that year Tom asked how long I thought it would take for the radio ministry to fund itself, and I told him about two years, but we needed to test the plausibility of the idea by asking listeners to financially sustain us. We held our first pledge drive in the fall of 2002, and the listeners made it abundantly clear that they were willing to support the apostolate.

In February 2003 I was attacked by necrotizing fasciitis, a flesh-eating bacteria, and lost my left leg. I was unable to return to work for six months, but during that time Tom ensured that our living quarters and studios would be adapted for a wheelchair. He also gave reassurances to me and my staff that we would get through this, and not to worry about meeting some of the deadlines we had earlier established.

Tom's philanthropic interests had been sharpening as his plans for a university evolved. He divested himself of several of his enterprises and pushed others toward financial independence, finally announcing that his main focus would be on Ave Maria University, which he established in southwest Florida near Naples. He continued to show interest in the radio work but ceased any direct financial contribution, which was not done abruptly, but in concert with us over a two-and-half-year period. While we continue to enjoy some budgetary advantages through our affiliation with his foundation (such as getting a favorable lease rate at Domino's Farms and participating in the employee benefit program), we are essentially on our own in meeting our operational needs.

Ave Maria programming has continued to grow and is now heard on 250 Catholic stations around the country, as well as Sirius satellite radio. We have a close relationship with EWTN and currently provide over three hours of programming for them weekdays as well. Now in our fifteenth year, we continue to be listener supported as well as receiving some corporate underwriting that we've developed. Not a day goes by that we don't hear some story of a life that's been changed, someone who has some false notion corrected, a marriage that found new stability, or a young man or woman who hears a call to religious life through Catholic radio. We've also helped to create the Catholic Radio Association, which is the "trade" organization for the 160 or so Catholic radio stations and, of course, stayed current with websites, blogs, apps for iPhones and Droid, streaming audio, as well as delivering our programming through satellite.

Tom was a great help to me in that he had failed so often, even sharing these stories with our staff early on. A person who tries much is going to fail much, but some things will succeed as long as one continues on courageously and keeps learning. Watching him risk his personal comfort and affluence for the sake of the Kingdom and then seeing how his successes have benefited so many remains an important life lesson for me.

Tom had been involved on many school boards, such as Catholic University of America and Franciscan University of Steubenville, as well as Fr. Gabriel Richard High School in Ann Arbor. By participating on these boards he saw the transformation that could take place when a school had a board committed to holding fast to principles that promoted the faith in a profound way. He became involved in a grade school called St. Michael's Academy in Ann Arbor that was started by a group of parents who were seeking an authentic Catholic education for their children and had developed a new concept of a privately run school. The school had approximately 70-80 students, who were getting a good education, but they were struggling financially, so they asked for Tom's support. In 1995 the school was renamed Spiritus Sanctus Academy (Latin for Holy Spirit) and Tom built them a new school adjacent to Domino's Farms. He also began looking for Catholic teachers who could help.

Around that same time Mother Assumpta Long was also feeling a call to start a new teaching order. Inspired by John Paul II's call to a "new evangelization" and his request for a renewal in religious life, Mother Assumpta and three other sisters left the Nashville-based Dominican order of St. Cecilia to embark on a new mission. On February 9, 1997, Cardinal John O'Connor established the rite for this new order, Dominican Sisters of Mary Mother of the Eucharist at St. Patrick's Cathedral in New York. "We are consecrated women first, and so our foremost model is Mary, the Mother of God. Inspired by the charism of St. Dominic, our prayer life comes first so that our apostolate overflows from a contemplation nourished before the Eucharist." This commitment explains their success. Starting with only four sisters, their order has now become the fastest growing and youngest order in the United States, with the average age of the women entering at 21. Recently, it was even featured on the *Oprah* program, enabling viewers to get a firsthand look at religious life. Tom spoke to Cardinal O'Connor and Mother Assumpta about his plan to have religious sisters teaching at the Spiritus Sanctus school, and after receiving the blessing of Bishop Mengling from the local Diocese of Lansing, Mother Assumpta began working at establishing a Mother house several miles from Domino's Farms.

This special teaching order of sisters has now flourished, and these sisters are found throughout the country, including the town of Ave Maria, where they live and teach at the Rhodora J. Donahue Academy K-12 School. Wearing their white Dominican habits, they can easily be spotted around the campus and town. It is their beautiful smile that is the most attractive and radiates Christ to their students, those who visit Ave Maria, and all those whom they encounter.

MOTHER MARY ASSUMPTA LONG, O.P.: PRIORESS GENERAL, SISTERS OF MARY MOTHER OF THE EUCHARIST

In July of 1996, Sr. Joseph Andrew, Sr. Mary Samuel, Sr. John Dominic, and I were driving to New York to begin a period of discernment in the Archdiocese of New York, under the direction of John Cardinal O'Connor, for the possibility of making a new religious foundation, which would be named The Dominican Sisters of Mary, Mother of the Eucharist. In God's providence—something He knew but would later become a surprise to us—we drove through Chicago, Illinois, and en route one of the sisters purchased a copy of USA Today, *which happened to be featuring an article on Tom Monaghan, and brought this great man to our thoughts. While studying the atlas, we realized that Ann Arbor might be doable toward our New York destination and thus decided to stop in the land of the Wolverines in hopes that Mr. Monaghan would be in town. Tom and I had known each other for some years and shared a deep love for the Catholic faith and a common zeal for spreading the Church's Truths. The sisters were blessed to meet him for only a brief time, but that short visit would, unknown to us, have a major influence on the future of our Community.*

Our journey successfully took us to New York, wherein shortly after our arrival, a phone call surprised us—it was from Tom. He began sharing his vision of building small Catholic Schools which he would, most willingly, give to our Sisters. Needless to say, I phoned John Cardinal O'Connor to seek his direction as Tom, never being one to waste a moment, had already given me a peek into a vast plan of his. The Cardinal prudently advised us to remain open while listening to Tom's thoughts and certainly praying over the situation. Tom then flew out to New York and, in our meeting, I explained the primary need for a Motherhouse after the Community would be canonically established. Tom—in his customary undeterred manner—answered that this made total sense to him, and he wished to assist us with the financial needs of such an endeavor. Should God truly will our "new Community," Mr. Monaghan was offering his assistance on many levels. He hoped, of course, that the Community would be moved to Ann Arbor, as his vision of Catholic education was one that burned deeply in his heart through ideas by which he might help our sisters bring the Faith to countless students in future years. Of course, we both had to learn about each other's world—Tom is an astute businessman and I have spent my entire religious life seeking to understand and preserve the Church's directives. While we struggled to see each other's perspective, I can honestly say I never once questioned his intentions and have always had a deep and profound admiration of him. It is without a doubt that Tom's faith and willingness to journey with us enabled the Dominican Sisters of Mary to begin with a solid foundation.

Tom's plan was to start with elementary schools and from there develop high schools and eventually a college, but he knew he couldn't do it all. When Tom succeeded at Domino's it was largely because he stayed focused. Domino's had one product—pizza—and only one business, pizza delivery stores. He believed it was that focus that was the key to Domino's achieving its goals. Applying these same business principles, he decided that if he was going to have the greatest impact in the educational arena, that he should focus his resources in higher education. The higher education level was by far the most expensive and complicated to set up, but it was also the most important, because graduates with strong foundations could have the greatest impact on the family, society, and the Church.

Parents' wedding 1936

Tom at age four when his father died.

Sr. Mary Berada

Seventh grade photo at Immaculate Conception School

Tom with classmates at St. Francis High School.

Proud to be a Marine.

Domino's Pizza Cross Street store.

Early Domino days.

Flipping pizzas at Pizza King.

The Domino's Pizza box

Wedding Day 1962

Detroit Tigers and Tom

Tom in the Detroit Tigers dugout.

John Paul II and Tom

Mother Angelica

Cardinal John O'Connor and Dominican Sisters
of Mary Mother of the Eucharist

CHAPTER FIVE

From the Heart of the Church

"I am the way and the truth and the life.
No one comes to the Father except through me."
JOHN 14:6

Many Catholics today can remember a time when seminaries and convents were full, Catholics did not divorce, and the Mass and the Sacraments were a vital part of spiritual life. By the 1960's the Church most of us knew had become almost unrecognizable. The seminaries were waning as good men were no longer answering the call to serve in the priesthood mostly due to their own lack of spiritual formation as well as the disorder that had infiltrated many of their walls at that time. Mass attendance had also dropped as "fallen away" Catholics quickly became the number two religious group in America, and Catholic politicians began to shamefully take their place as leaders in the assault against human life.

On July 23, 1967 in Land O' Lakes, Wisconsin, twenty six Catholic leaders from ten Catholic colleges and universities from across the country met at what has now become known as the Land O' Lakes Conference. Wishing to portray themselves as academically superior to gain social recognition with other secular institutions, they declared their independence from any outside authority including the Catholic Church stating:

The Catholic University today must be a university in the full modern sense of the word, with a strong commitment to and concern for academic excellence. To perform its teaching and research functions effectively the Catholic university must have a <u>*true autonomy and academic freedom in the face of authority of whatever kind, lay or clerical, external to the academic community itself.*</u> *To say this is simply to assert that institutional autonomy and academic freedom are essential conditions of life and growth and indeed of survival for Catholic universities as for all universities.-* **Statement on the Nature of the Contemporary Catholic University**

In the subsequent years following this conference, most of these Catholic institutions turned away from virtually any Catholic identity at all, drifting more and more toward moral and social relativism, with less regard for religious truth. Many hired faculty without any consideration of their faith or support of Catholic higher education, and by separating "faith" from "reason" they created a vacuum that encouraged a new relativism based on academic freedom and little concern for an authentic search for truth.

Sadly, it dawned on Tom that many Catholics had no foundation for knowing their faith. He could give his money to worthy causes like cancer or heart disease, but if those people died and lost their souls to hell for all eternity, what good would it do?

It would take more than good catechesis to meet these goals, but the truths of the faith needed to be integrated into every aspect of education, including social, cultural, economic, and political disciplines. This was crucial because as Catholic universities were losing their identity, the whole world was suffering. *This became his reason for founding Ave Maria University, and the timing was right!*

By 1990 Pope John Paul II issued an "apostolic constitution" titled *Ex corde Ecclesiae* (From the Heart of the Church), which cleared up the confusion created by the Land O' Lakes Conference, and he established guidelines to reaffirm the Catholic identity of a university, stating:

> ***BORN FROM THE HEART*** *of the Church, a Catholic University is located in that course of tradition which may be traced back to the very origin of the University as an institution. It has always been recognized as an incomparable centre of creativity and dissemination of knowledge for the good of humanity. By vocation, the Universitas magistrorum et scholarium is dedicated to research, to teaching and to the education of students who freely associate with their teachers in a common love of knowledge. With every other University it shares that gaudium de veritate, so precious to Saint Augustine, which is that joy of searching for, discovering and communicating truth in every field of knowledge. A Catholic University's privileged task is "to unite existentially by intellectual effort two orders of reality that too frequently tend to be placed in opposition as though they were antithetical: the search for truth, and the certainty of already knowing the fount of truth". - Ex corde Ecclesiae*

In this document, Pope John Paul II proposed that a Catholic university reflect fidelity to the Magisterium of the Church in all its actions, that it was the responsibility of the faculty and administrators to respect that identity and teach in accordance with it, and that the majority of those teaching at that institution be Catholic. This document established new hope of renewal and reform in Catholic universities, and it was just in time for the influx of JP II youth, who were hungry to live out their faith.

In 1993 at the World Youth Day in Denver's Mile High Stadium, the Pope addressed a half million young people with this message "Jesus has called each one of you to Denver for a purpose. You must live these days in such a way that, when the time comes to return home, each one of you will have a clearer idea of what Christ expects of you. Each one must have the courage to go and spread the Good News ... among young people of your own age, who will take the church and society into the next century." Countless young people left that stadium that day in search of a way to live out that call and begin their own journey in faith, and for many of these young people and their families, Ave Maria would be their answer. As Fr. Richard John Neuhaus said before his death, "The Church is not as good as it was 40 years ago, but better than it was 10 years ago." We have seen what a world and Church looks like when we turn our back on God, and now the pendulum was swinging again, but this time in the right direction!

CHAPTER SIX

Giving Birth to a Catholic University

"We know that all things work for good for those who love God, who are called according to His purpose."
ROMANS 8:28

Tom had been on six college and university boards, so he was getting a feel for academia and knew there were only a handful remaining that were solidly faithful. He was on the board of Franciscan University in Steubenville, Ohio and believed that Franciscan, through the leadership of Fr. Michael Scanlan, was one of the best examples of taking a mediocre Catholic institution and reviving it through authentic Catholic teaching.

In 1996 an organization called Christus Magister (Christ the Teacher) was introduced by Nick Healy, who was then the Vice President of University Relations at Franciscan University, and largely responsible for the successful conference programs that we know today. The FUS summer youth programs had grown exponentially, so they began to look at other areas of the country in which to expand, and found great support by fellow Catholics in the Phoenix, Arizona area, which was also home to the Life Teen movement. Building on that winning formula for growing youth conferences, Nick Healy had the idea that they could do the same with the university and establish more FUS type schools across the country starting first in Phoenix, where they had this great support. He spoke with FUS President, Fr. Michael Scanlan, about the idea, and Fr. Scanlan was very encouraging, but concerned about the financial and management issues of having a school at such a distance, so they agreed instead to set up an independent foundation (Christus Magister) allowing the FUS to be its mentor and guide.

They put together a top-notch board that included Fr. Michael Scanlan, President of FUS; Dr. Michael J. Healy; Dr. David Schindler, Dean of the John Paul II Institute in Washington DC; Mary Ann Glendon, Kenneth Whitehead; Ralph Martin; Fr Joseph Fessio S.J.; Archbishop Charles Chaput; James Holman; Tom Monaghan; Nick Healy; and Fr. Benedict Groeschel, C.F.R; who was also responsible for the Christus Magister name. Money quickly came in from donors who were excited about the vision, and with the blessing of the local bishop and Ex Corde Ecclesia already implemented by the Church just a few years before, they were ready to put together a program that included strong academics, a great student life program, and a faculty that would reflect the beauty of the faith. Nick organized some parent meetings and helped with the interviewing of the new president.

Shortly afterwards, Nick learned that the bishop of Phoenix had changed his mind and was withdrawing his support. By this time, however, the vision of Christus Magister had already gotten out and there was interest in other parts of the country, which made Tom Monaghan think, why not start a school in Michigan? Tom had always been big on franchising and saw starting new schools like Franciscan as crucial to restoring the Catholic faith in our youth, which would in turn revitalize the Church. In the beginning they had to start small, but his goal was to grow the college over time and someday locate it within Domino's Farms.

Ave Maria College opened its doors in the fall of 1998, but in the beginning could only be called an "institute" until it received the necessary charter from the State of Michigan to be called a college. The name "Ave Maria" was chosen because it was recognizable for many of the same reasons that the foundation was named earlier, but most importantly so it would remain always under Our Lady's heavenly mantle. Many would refer to Ave Maria in the years to come as the "bubble" that kept the "real world" out, but for those who have been blessed to be part of it, they would say it is more like a womb where Our Blessed Mother nurtures, God the Father protects, Jesus provides, and the Holy Spirit gives birth to lives ready to serve the Lord!

Soon the search was on for a president. Nick Healy, VP of University Relations at Franciscan University (FUS), suggested Dr. Michael J. Healy, the Dean of Faculty (at FUS), but no relation to Nick, for president of Ave Maria Institute. Dr. Healy had served as Academic Dean under Fr. Michael Scanlan and was on the Christus Magister board. Mike Healy suggested Dr. Ron Muller instead; he had been at the University of Dallas and was the co-founder of a very small school in Fort Worth, Texas called St. Thomas More.

Dr. Muller and Tom then met with Bishop Mengeling, the newly appointed Bishop of Lansing, who was also a former professor and highly interested in education. He was tentative about the new school at first and asked a lot of questions, but Ron Muller was a veteran and also very qualified, so the answers he gave met the approval of the bishop. Ron was then hired as the first provost, and he began the administrative duties of the institute. The key was that FUS was allowed to oversee the development of the curriculum at Ave Maria Institute, and guaranteed if any student wanted to transfer to FUS, that their credits would be accepted at FUS—an arrangement that had the support of Fr. Scanlan and Mike Healy.

Starting with only 10 full time students and eight part time students, Tom bolstered the numbers by offering free classes in theology and philosophy to Domino's Farm employees, with classes held in the cafeteria. Tom even took classes himself. The first graduating class totaled seven students, all transfers, four boys' and three girls' with three of the four going into the seminary!

MOST REV. CARL F. MENGELING, BISHOP EMERITUS FOR THE DIOCESE OF LANSING: "ON FIRE FOR CATHOLIC EDUCATION"

Back in 1996 this new bishop, who was also new to Michigan, was visited by an unknown guest, Tom Monaghan, who spoke kindly and frankly about his own story and his plans for Catholic education. It was with relief and joy that, through our conversation, I soon realized that this plan was a common vision that we both shared! Of course, we were like minded about our Catholic faith, but particularly about the final words of Jesus to the first evangelizers, who were commanded in Matthew 28:19, to "Go! Teach!" What a blessing this was for a baby bishop!

Tom frequently spoke of the great education that he received in the Catholic schools and how thankful he was to the religious sisters who taught him. This is how he first got the "bug" to become involved in Catholic education, and his plan was to assist Catholic elementary schools and a community of religious sisters to teach. In 1997 four Dominican sisters arrived in Ann Arbor, and Tom provided them with the land, a residence, and even more; he sustained them. They soon went on to establish several other local schools and today there are more than 120 Sisters of Mary Mother of the Eucharist who teach in many cities throughout the United States.

Tom also joined the region wide Catholic effort for a new Gabriel Richard High School. He cinched the drive for the new school by donating the 40 acres in which to build it, and made a significant gift toward the building campaign. Gabriel Richard High School is now a Catholic High School with full enrollment and waiting lists.

The courageous and remarkable saga of Ave Maria University found its center in Ypsilanti, and I will never forget the first dedication and procession of faculty and students. These were the future greats who were on their way, and with them much hope and enthusiasm for the future. That future is now in full swing at Ave Maria University in Florida.

Tom is appreciated and will always be remembered for his dynamic vision for Catholic Schools. Whether it was local or nationwide elementary schools, the religious sisters of St. Dominic, Father Gabriel Richard High School, or Ave Maria University, he was fulfilling the call to "Go! Teach!"

In late 1998, after 38 years of business, Tom sold Domino's pizza to Bain Capital, an investment firm based in Boston, for an estimated $1 billion. He was 61 years old. With the sale of Domino's came a major boost in the resources needed to move forward with the college and other foundation projects. When he was asked if he would miss Domino's, he said that he was, truthfully, relieved. He said that Ray Kroc (Mc Donald's CEO and Founder) had a poster about "Persistence" that said persistence was more important than any other ingredient in being successful, more important than genius, and even more important than hard work. He believed that this was a quality that he had, that he was "too dumb to quit." Domino's had provided a good life for Tom and his family, and now through its sale it would provide for others. After selling Domino's he was looking ahead to full time charitable work and he never looked back.

In 1999, just after selling Domino's, one of the projects Tom began working on was a movie on the life of Pope John Paul II who was still living at this time and a great hero of his. Pope John Paul's life was a dramatic story filled with many trials and tribulations as well as being the ultimate story of faith. Tom contacted Cardinal Adam Joseph Maida (then the Archbishop of Detroit), who approached the Vatican about the idea, and he was given the approval to proceed. The film had a $55 million budget, and Tom already had $5 million invested in it when they started to run into problems. After a year of working on the film and doing some initial site work in Poland and Rome, he was starting to get frustrated with the Hollywood types and many of the irregularities that he saw. Around this same time Archbishop John Foley (who later became Cardinal Foley and who was the President of Pontifical Council for Social Communications for the Vatican) contacted him and asked that they stop the movie. Even though Tom already had a lot invested in the film, his feeling was that if Rome said no, he would not do it. He hadn't signed the contract yet, so after hearing of Rome's decision he canceled the film.

In the middle of all of this Tom was contacted by Raymond Arroyo from EWTN *The World Over* about investing in a movie that Mel

Gibson was going to direct, *The Passion of the Christ*. Arroyo set up a meeting in Los Angeles with Gibson and actor Jim Caviezel, who would portray Jesus, to discuss the investment opportunity. Gibson was very animated, with his hands darting around, as he showed them some video footage shot in the southern Italian town where they were going to film. They were surprised to learn that there would be no English in the movie and that he would be using two dead languages in its filming, but this was something they felt they could overlook. Paul Roney (former CFO of AMU and Executive Director of the Ave Maria Foundation), who was also at that meeting, said he was intrigued by Gibson's expressive blue eyes, and he thought that Caviezel had almost a mystical quality about him.

The film was budgeted at $20 million, and they were asking for a $7 million investment from Tom for 35 percent of the movie profits. However, with all the problems he already had with the John Paul II movie and recent experience with Hollywood, he turned the opportunity down.

The final cost of the movie was $30 million, with an estimated $15 million spent on marketing the film, and Gibson and his company, Icon Productions, ended up providing the sole backing. The movie was released in 2004 and was a major hit, making $600 million at the box office and an estimated total of $800 million in sales. Tom said he can only think now of all the good that money could have done for Ave Maria University but in the end he was pleased that Mel was able to reach so many souls for God through it. This decision became one of the greatest financial regrets of his life.

By 1999 Ave Maria Institute received permission from the state to be called a college, and Nick Healy was brought in to replace Ron Muller in the interim as they searched for a president. Tom and Fr. Fessio had been working on a radio project in California, and Tom asked him who he thought would be a good president for the college. Fr. Fessio responded by telling him that Mike Healy would be a good choice, and if he couldn't do it, "get the other Healy"—meaning Nick. Nick by this time was just retiring from FUS and was planning on living with his wife Jane in their dream home that they had built in New Hampshire. Tom asked Nick to come oversee the college for just one year, which he agreed to do, leaving his wife Jane behind in New Hampshire as he commuted home on weekends. During that year Nick brought Tom many new candidates, but Tom didn't seem to show any serious interest in them. One candidate did seem to be a perfect fit, but he declined the position. By the second year they had stopped looking, and Tom asked Nick to take the position. In 2000 Nick Healy became Ave Maria College's first president, and his wife Jane moved to Ypsilanti to join him. When asked how they were able to discern taking the new job and making the move, Nick explained that he and Jane just had a sense when something was in God's plan.

NICHOLAS J. HEALY: FIRST PRESIDENT OF AVE MARIA COLLEGE, AVE MARIA UNIVERSITY

I first met Tom Monaghan when he came to Franciscan University to give a talk. He arrived on campus via helicopter with a squad of security and aides de camp. His newest acquisition, the Detroit Tigers, had won the World Series and Tom was at the peak of success. I doubt there would have been more excitement on the campus if President Reagan had arrived. Yet even then he showed a streak of humility and an underlying devotion to the Catholic Church. Both of these attributes became more manifest in subsequent years.

Tom and I served together as Trustees of Franciscan from 1985 on. Tom's admiration for Fr. Michael Scanlan, T.O.R., the President of Franciscan University, knew no bounds. He said many times, after the establishment of Ave Maria College and University, "Franciscan University is our model, and Fr. Scanlan is my hero."

In the mid 1990s, long after I had joined FUS as an administrator, I initiated a project to help foster new Catholic colleges. Tom joined the board of the foundation, leading this effort. When he heard the outline of how a new college could be started, his immediate reaction was "I want to do one of those!" Thus was born the plan for Ave Maria College in Ypsi-lanti, Michigan, which became the genesis for Ave Maria University. After its first year, Tom asked me to be "interim" president while a search was made for an experienced academic. However in a few months Tom and I developed a working relationship that led to my staying on for twelve years. Being the first president of Ave Maria College and of Ave Maria University was both a surprise and an honor for me.

Often when one works closely with another, the flaws and deficiencies become more obvious, and perhaps more difficult to accept; certainly Tom has flaws and weaknesses, but they are pretty obvious. What I found was that as I got to know Tom better, I kept finding new depths of character and virtue, a piety that is astonishing in its discipline, and commitment to sacrifice, much of it hidden and practiced seemingly effortlessly.

The establishment of a new Catholic institution of higher learning is daunting. The expectations of those involved, faculty, staff, trustees, do-nors, students, always seem unrealistic, perhaps inspired by the nobility of the effort and the sense of great importance. When the expectations are not realized, or when policies are implemented that seem at odds with the ex-alted goals, the reactions can be fierce—and disproportionate. Through the turmoil of the early years especially, we all had to endure harsh criticism, often in the media. Tom always had to take the brunt of it. I often won-dered whether Tom would get to the point of saying "enough" and simply withdraw to a more relaxed life with his family and friends. No doubt a lesser man would have. Yet Tom seemed to take the punishment as a kind of penance. Never once was there anything but a steely resolution to see it through, no matter what insults or slanders were directed toward him. No doubt this was in large part due to his Marine Corps training, and deep admiration for soldierly discipline.

It is a remarkable fact that there are no buildings or even rooms named for Tom Monaghan. If decades from now he is remembered for founding Ave Maria University, it will not be because he planned it or even expected it. Rather, it will be because of the mysterious ways of the Divine to bring to light the good deeds of His servants at the appropriate hour. We have His promise it will be done: "He who honors Me, I will honor" (1 Samuel 2:30).

It has been a privilege to walk side by side with this remarkable man for many years. I pray our paths will converge again.

They received a few transfers students from Franciscan University, and enrollment continued to grow, especially after the sale of Domino's, which gave them the extra resources to provide many scholarships to the students who attended. Ralph Martin from Renewal Ministries, who did a lot of work in Eastern Europe after the fall of the Soviet Union, recruited students, as did Jenny Healy, Nick's daughter, who was part of the Language and Catechetical Institute (LCI) in Austria.

As the school grew, they purchased an apartment building as well as a few older homes on the block that they refurbished to house the students. Together, the Healys spruced up the drab campus with landscaping and paint that made it rather charming, a sort of oasis right next to the campus of Eastern Michigan University. Ave Maria students joined other students from Eastern Michigan University at the Newman Center, and this brought opportunities to serve and to do ministry work on their campus too.

The Ypsilanti campus was also attracting excellent faculty, as there were many good Catholics who wanted to unabashedly profess their faith, and for them Ave Maria was a good fit of faith, family, and profession. As well as hiring exceptional faculty, the college was able to establish an incredible library. Dr. Thomas Loome, along with his wife Karen, founded the Loome Theological Booksellers in Stillwater, Minnesota. They had the foresight early on to collect books from seminaries and religious houses that were closing in the late '60s and early '70s and their collection became a great source of books for Ave Maria, especially in theology, philosophy, history, and biblical studies. In 2007 the Aquinas Center for Theological Renewal at Ave Maria University honored Dr. Loome with the Ex Corde Ecclesiae Medal for his work on the library and support of students in the Graduate Program in Theology. The library currently serves both the students and faculty today at AMU and has become a great foundation on which the university can build as it continues to grow.

As Ave Maria College was being launched, Tom was also busy with the Ave Maria School of Law that had opened its doors in 2000 in Ann Arbor, several miles from Domino's Farms. When Tom was on the board of FUS, the case was made that there was a real need for an authentically Catholic law school. At one point, the suggestion was that maybe Franciscan University leaders would like to start a law school but they declined saying they wanted to stay focused on the curriculum that was already in place. Tom wanted to continue to pursue the idea because he believed that lawyers could have such a big influence on Supreme Court issues and on society, as politicians, judges, and in the corporate world. In the early '90s before the sale of Domino's, he wrote a check to encourage others to do some exploratory work on the feasibility of opening one in the future. He continued to keep the idea of a law school in mind so that later when the opportunity did present itself again and he was financially able to do something about it, he was ready.

Ave Maria School of Law had an outstanding faculty and board that included Cardinal O'Connor, Fr. Michael Scanlan, Judge Jim Ryan, Charlie Rice, Judge and United States Senator Jim Buckley, Judge Bill Clark (President Reagan's top aide), Helen Alvare', Kate O' Beirne, Cardinal Maida, Fr. Joseph Fessio, Robert George, Teresa Collett, Gerry Bradley, Dean Bernard Dobranski, and Tom Monaghan as the chairman and founder.

As the search began for faculty, Richard Thompson was able to make a few suggestions to assist Tom in this endeavor. Richard Thompson always had a passion for pro-life and pro-family causes and had proposed a not-for-profit organization that could provide legal representation without charge to defend Christians and their religious liberties in the public square. Thompson spent 24 years of his professional career at the executive level of law enforcement and as the elected Oakland County, Michigan Prosecuting Attorney (from 1989 to 1996). He gained national recognition as the prosecuting attorney that took on Jack Kevorkian (Dr. Death) and Physician Assisted Suicide in the state of Michigan.

Tom was totally supportive and offered the initial funding in 1999 for what was to be appropriately named the Thomas More Law Center. Sir Thomas More was the famous 16th century Chancellor of England who was beheaded because of his faith. Before he died he humbly described himself as the "King's good servant, but God's first," and in 1935 was canonized a saint by the Catholic Church.

On an average the TMLC can have over 100 open cases in numerous states and dozens more in active litigation in the courts. Most recently it was the TMLC that challenged the constitutionality of ObamaCare. Although it was dismissed by the U.S. District Court, TMLC filed an appeal to the U.S. Court of Appeals and may very well become the first case to reach the U.S. Supreme Court on this issue. The Thomas More Law Center has been involved in numerous other cases through the years that have received national attention, such as the Terri Schiavo case, the removal of the Mt. Soledad cross in California, and defending Alabama Chief Judge Roy Moore when he was ordered to remove the Ten Commandments from the state's Supreme Court Building. The TMLC also defended Lt. Col. Jeffrey Chessani, who was criminally charged for the legitimate combat action taken by four of his Marines who were ambushed by insurgents in Iraq in 2005, and whose case was made the political scapegoat by anti-war politicians and the liberal media as well as many other cases. The Thomas More Law Center continues to actively work toward preventing the erosion of so many of the values, rights, and freedoms that our country was founded on, and their contribution is vitally important during these critical times in which we live.

An attractive Alden Dow (student of Frank Lloyd Wright) building was purchased in Ann Arbor, and architect David Uppgren adapted it into the new law school. The plan was to later move it to Domino's Farms, where Tom also planned on moving Ave Maria College someday.

Another first in 2000 was the Pre-Theologate program. Fr. Dave Testa, a diocesan priest from Albany, N.Y., joined the staff at Ave Maria to start this program that assisted young men in discerning religious life. Continuing a program that he had successfully started at Franciscan University just five years before, it encompassed the same coursework in philosophy and theology required to enter a major seminary while at the same time allowing the men to take classes on a coed campus. During this time these young men were able to live the life of discernment as they attended daily Mass together, recited the Liturgy of the Hours, and developed a unified brotherhood, and with only a semester to semester commitment. If they decided during that time that the priesthood was not their vocation, they could withdraw. The program was a success either way because whether they chose the priesthood or not, they had a chance for solid formation in the faith.

"Every year young men graduating from high school are thinking about the priesthood but are not ready to make a commitment to the seminary. So they get a job, go to college, join the military, etc. These options are not necessarily supportive of a possible vocation," Fr. Testa said. "A college-level pre-theologate is made for these young men, allowing them to be ordinary college students, and majoring in the field of their choice with very little pressure." Years later, when he saw these young men again, they thanked him for the formation they received and said that the time they spent in prayer and discernment made a big difference in their lives. Many young men did answer the call through this unique opportunity, but whether they chose the priesthood or not the program produced good, solid Catholic men who knew their faith and were willing to take it wherever the Lord led them.

Fr. Dave Testa succumbed to cancer and died on June 6, 2002, just a few short years after beginning the program at Ave Maria. "My dream would be to see pre-theologate Programs at Catholic universities around the country. The Church has a critical need for priestly vocations and, I believe with all my heart, this program saves and nurtures future vocations among men who are not ready to commit their lives to a seminary. May God strengthen and encourage all of us in reaching this dream," he stated, and profoundly so, not long before his death. Fr. Ed Fride, the pastor at Christ the King parish in Ann Arbor, then became the program's successor and continued to provide the rich soil on which these future vocations could fostered.

FR. JOSEPH BAMBENEK, PASTOR: POPE PIUS X PARISH, WHITE BEAR LAKE, MINNESOTA

Fr. Joseph Bambenek's journey began at Ave Maria College (AMC) in Ypsilanti, Michigan several years before the move to Florida. As a young man in his early 30s he already had a solid career and a double Master's degree in engineering before he made a decision to follow God's call. This decision was an outgrowth of having grown spiritually through the Franciscan University (FUS) programs that he had attended in the past. Working for an energy company in Jackson, Michigan, he was transferred to Ann Arbor when, through a gift he gave to the school in honor of his parents, he was contacted by Dr. Carole Carpenter, from whom he first learned about the personal enrichment programs that the college offered, and began taking classes.

That same summer he explored the possibility of the priesthood and met with the vocations director in his home state of Minnesota; the director gave him the option of taking his prerequisite courses in philosophy and theology at AMC, which he did part time as he continued to work and live off campus. By 2003 Joseph was confident of his call and, in time, was invited to participate in the discernment talks, prayers, and discussions that were being offered by Fr. Ed Fride, the director of the Pre-Theologate. Through this program he found the formational support that he was searching for; consequently, he decided to give up his career and apartment and, at the age of 35, he moved into the dorm with seven other young men who were in the discernment program and whose average age was 21. Of the eight men total in the program, four of them have since become priests. Looking back, he said it was "providential" that he remained at AMC instead of going directly to the seminary for classes because of the tremendous influence those professors continue to have on his priestly life today.

The impact that he had on the college during his time at AMC was also a work of the Holy Spirit. He started a group called Reflect in the Diocese of Lansing for single Catholics that is still in existence today, and another called the Society of St. Margaret Cortona. This society was for Catholic single mothers. He was also the last student government president of the Michigan campus and came to recognize ever more deeply the importance of forgiveness during the challenging time of transition when the decision was made to move Ave Maria College to Naples, Florida. During deep, searching prayer, he was led to St. Maria Goretti, whose life was a powerful witness of forgiveness and conversion and, through her intercession, many found the means to reconciliation.

In 2010 Fr. Bambenek was ordained a priest in the Archdiocese of St. Paul and Minneapolis, and on March 25, 2011 he attended the unveiling of the Annunciation sculpture that covers the façade of the Oratory. The day before, he celebrated a Mass of Thanksgiving in the Ave Maria Oratory, and looking out on the impressive numbers who were in attendance that day, he addressed his vocational journey by concluding:

> *My hope and prayer is that each of the students here at Ave Maria, and for that matter all who are here today to celebrate Mass, will open your hearts ever more fully to what God wants to teach you, to how God wants to work through you, so that someday you are able to return here in one way or another and testify to how, during your years at Ave Maria, you were well prepared for fulfilling the wonderful vocation that God has lovingly given you, whatever that might be. Furthermore, let us leave here today resolved to follow in the footsteps of Jesus, and of His modern disciple St. Maria Goretti. Let us follow the example of forgiveness; let us follow the example of purity. With our minds and hearts formed by what we have learned at Ave Maria, let us be joyful and forgiving instruments and witnesses of God's faith, hope, and love to all who we meet.*

In the summer of 2000 Ave Maria College acquired a campus in San Marcos, Nicaragua and named it Ave Maria College of the Americas. Tom had funded the building of the Cathedral in Managua in the early '90s so he already had some background in the country. The campus had originally been under the University of Mobile (Alabama) and was unique in that it provided an American degree, something that was desirable to Latin Americans and this could be done without the cost of going to the U.S. to obtain it. In 2007 the name of the college changed again, to Ave Maria University Latin American Campus, when it became a branch of the Ave Maria University in Florida. In 2013 Ave Maria College of the Americas was sold to Keiser University. At the celebration in late February of 2013, Keiser University Chancellor Arthur Keiser pledged to beautify the campus, to retain all faculty and staff who wished to stay, to establish programs abroad for the students, and to keep the culture and identity of the campus Catholic. "It started out as kind of a sad day for Ave Maria," said Richard Hailer, an Ave Maria resident who attended the ceremony. "But it turned joyful with Dr. Keiser's announcement that he would guarantee that the campus would keep its Catholic identity—which prompted cheers and a standing ovation from students and parents." Dr. Keiser also recognized Tom Monaghan, Gigi Daniels, and Henry Howard, who were long-time supporters, through sculptured busts that will remain in the school's new library. These gifts will become symbols and a testimony to the founders, who helped to establish this great work of evangelism in the Americas.

Ave Maria College offered programs that allowed the students on the Ypsilanti campus an opportunity to study abroad both in Nicaragua and also in Gaming, Austria. The Gaming, Austria program was one that Nick Healy had first initiated at Franciscan with Cardinal Christoph Schönborn. Through this program, students were able to immerse themselves in the fullness of the Church through their studies in Latin America and Europe and learn how the truths of the Church were being lived out in other cultures.

By 2001 the number of students at Ave Maria College had grown to more than 200. As the Ypsilanti campus grew, his plans of moving the campus to Domino's Farms were foremost in Tom's mind. What better place to integrate students in their spiritual, academic, and business functions than by putting them under the same roof? This would be great exposure for the students by allowing them to gain practical work experience in the complex that housed Domino's Pizza's headquarters and thirty other tenant companies and for their employees, who would benefit by having the campus and all it offered so close. The plan was a good one, but to get the needed zoning from Ann Arbor Township turned out to be too much. When all seemed lost, Tom did what he knew best: he asked Our Lady for her help.

CHAPTER SEVEN

The Move to Florida

*"Faith is the realization of what is hoped for
and evidence of things not yet seen."*
HEBREWS 11:1

In January of 2002, as Tom and his wife Margie were in Naples for their annual vacation after Christmas, he received that answer to his prayer. While in Naples he was having breakfast with two good friends, Fran Sehn and Pat O'Meara, and discussing the problems he was having in Michigan. The rezoning process was not going well in Ann Arbor. So Tom began thinking, *Why am I putting all this money into the Ann Arbor area? As long as I'm going through all this effort and expense, it might as well be in the best possible place, Naples, Florida!*

Tom was an avid demographics expert and had been plotting locations for stores and distribution centers around the country for Domino's for many years, so he didn't feel he needed to do a lot of study to support his idea. Clearly, Naples was the best area in the country. It had the best weather, with average temperatures between 75 and 80 degrees, and it would be a desirable location to attract both faculty and students from the entire country. During the time of year when most schools are in session and having inclement weather up north, Naples is the most beautiful!

Even more important, however, was the fact that there was a need for another Catholic college in the south. Ninety percent of Catholic colleges were founded in the north, with only nine in the south, and most of those were founded before air-conditioning was even invented! Tom discovered that there were only three Catholic colleges in Florida.

The next step toward exploring the move to Florida was getting the approval of the Bishop of the Venice Diocese in which Naples was located. Bishop Nevins couldn't have been more welcoming. He said in a February 2002 meeting that it would be a privilege to have a Catholic university within its province and called Ave Maria University "a great gift to the Diocese." Tom and the administration were met with the same enthusiasm from the chairman of the Collier County Board of Commissioners, Jim Coletta, who was ecstatic about the idea and whose response was, "What do we have to do to get you here?" The other four county commissioners were equally supportive. What a contrast to the circumstances that Tom had been dealing with in Ann Arbor. He had always envisioned the school being located in Ann Arbor and wanted to give his support there, but he finally came to the conclusion that every great movement or institution in the Church's history has always been met with enormous resistance in its early stages.

While still in the exploratory stages, the idea was presented to the Ave Maria College board, which supported the move, but with one important reservation. Their question to Tom was, "are you willing to commit your resources to this new venture?" They were concerned with future costs that were unknown at that time. The faculty also seemed supportive, overall, and the administration encouraged them to visit Naples so they could see the nature of the opportunity for themselves. Paul Roney, the CFO of the college, was also in favor of the move.

Ave Maria College was in the process of receiving national accreditation through North Central Association. With a move to Florida and the goal of becoming a university, the accreditation process would need to be started all over again with the Southern Association of Colleges and Schools (SACS) because of where it would be located. Therefore, the administration began working on a strategic plan to open the campus in Florida and wind down the campus in Michigan in a systematic and equitable way.

Dr. Michael Healy was the president of Ave Maria College in Michigan in 2002 for one academic year while President Nick Healy and his wife Jane moved to Florida to establish Ave Maria's presence there and begin the necessary accreditation work for the college. After Dr. Michael Healy's year as president, Dr. Ron Muller served as president until Dr. Dan Guernsey took over the closing phase.

Dr. Guernsey served as president and had the task of closing the college while at the same time providing for the best interests of the remaining students, faculty, and staff. The invitation was made to all faculty and students to transfer to the campus in Florida, but these were hard decisions for faculty and students who had family commitments, teenagers in school, housing issues, and other financial factors that would prevent them from moving immediately. Another big factor was the higher price of housing in Naples. Of the twelve faculty members that AMC had at that time, about half of them made the decision to stay in Michigan.

DR. DAN GUERNSEY, ED.D.: FORMER PRESIDENT OF AVE MARIA COLLEGE

The board had already decided to do whatever it took to do things right during the wind-down, and under the trajectory set in place before my arrival the college was poised to spend millions on the last two years of operation for just a few students. We re-examined operating assumptions and took the temperature of the College community and came up with a plan whereby we could move folks on with their lives with better opportunities and better use of resources by offering the faculty and students a type of buyout plan. In it, the student moved on to the college of their choice with a scholarship, and the faculty received a year's pay, without having to teach, thus allowing them to research and/or search for new placements. In the end, all faculty and all but five students were amenable to this idea.

Three of the five students were just holding out for larger scholarships, and two wanted to keep the college open for their final year, so in an amazing twist we decided to honor all the faculty salaries, all the transfer scholarships, and keep the college open for the five remaining holdouts. Three of those holdouts walked away with nothing, and of the two remaining hold outs one never fully returned in the fall, leaving us with just one student. Yes, we kept the college open just for her! A situation so unbelievable the Chronicle of Higher Education came out to do a story on us.

Going to such extreme lengths to keep one's word, even with some of those who at least at some level seemed be working against the vision and efforts of the board, is truly an amazing end to this first phase of the University's growth.

As Nick and Jane were getting settled in Naples, Nick began looking for available property to build AMU. By February of 2002 he contacted Ross McIntosh, a highly recommended Florida realtor, to assist him in finding a large piece of land. Tom wanted a minimum of 500 acres for the new campus to house the end goal of 5,000 students as well as a state-of-the-art golf course. Part of the original master plan for the campus in Ann Arbor was to have a course designed by the famous golf course architect Rees Jones and to have members from all over the world join as a sort of a Catholic Augusta National. Tom's thinking was that its members would get to know the students and the faculty, sponsor some of the academic programs, get involved with the sports at the university, and become lifelong donors to the university. He also planned on inviting bishops and cardinals to be ex-oficio members to play at no charge, and they could also stay on campus for a needed rest, retreat, or a private vacation.

Tom was willing to consider the right piece of property anywhere from Marco Island to Ft. Myers, but each one that was brought before him seemed to have its own set of problems. Then they found something that was way beyond all of their dreams.

The property was four sections; about 2,600 acres total with about

1,300 acres useable property and the rest wetlands. The acreage included four lakes that had been quarried for stone and gravel for years, and had space for a golf course and thousands of homes. It was more land than they needed, but the idea was to put the university in the center of it and maybe develop the remaining land to provide a great endowment for AMU. The property was in the northeast corner of Naples, which was something Tom found highly desirable due to its close proximity to Naples and all that it had to offer. The problem was the owner was already well down the road to developing this massive project and was eager to begin construction, so they had to move fast. This was now early April 2002.

Ensuing discussions with the owner took place and a deal was struck, but it would not be cheap and would take a great deal of Tom's liquid assets. A large deposit was made and a contract signed that contained only a thirty-day due diligence period that allowed them to inspect the property. During that time, if they found anything objectionable they could cancel without losing the deposit.

Now that they had the option on the land as well as the blessing of Bishop Nevins and the county commissioners, they were ready to come out publically and reveal their plan to the Naples community. They decided not to reveal that they had a site when making the public announcement in light of the due diligence contingency.

Following that public announcement and press conference, they received a call from the Barron Collier Company (BCC), who was the largest landowner in the county. Barron Collier was a pioneer and visionary who made his fortune selling advertisements on streetcars in New York. In 1911 he purchased 1.3 million acres of this proverbial Florida swampland, making him the largest landowner in the state. By 1923 he had established Collier County and in 1928 personally completed the Tamiami Trail which connected Naples to Miami. Paul Marinelli, the president of BCC, called to say that the Barron Collier Company had a piece of land 17 miles further inland of the quarry site and the company was offering AMU all the land free if they would build the university about 35 miles north and east of Naples on their site.

The Florida legislature had just passed a Rural Lands Stewardship initiative that created stewardship credits as an incentive to use the most sensitive lands as sending areas and the least sensitive as receiving areas that could be developed. Specifically the county's program was to protect the wildlife habitat, water flow ways, and other environmental resources in certain protected and agricultural areas while encouraging new growth in others which was a winning formula for developers and environmentalists alike. Naples had outgrown its space so the push had to be eastward and BCC envisioned a new town as a catalyst to that undeveloped land, with the university as its anchor, and the Rural Lands Stewardship as the means to make that happen.

Tom immediately rejected the offer because he felt it was too far out of Naples and by this time he was getting more and more excited about the quarry site. However, toward the end of the thirty-day due diligence period, something unexpected happened. Developers received word that an eagle was spotted with a twig in its mouth on the quarry site, which indicated there could be a nest. If a nest did exist on the site, they were suddenly going to be hit with all kinds of federally mandated restrictions. These restrictions included: no developing at all within the perimeter around the nest and limited development extending outside of the perimeter. It would also mean that the value of the property could be severely impacted, making it questionable to build the university there.

These events happened as their option was running out, so they asked for one more week of due diligence to determine whether there was a nest on the property or if it was a fluke. It was during this time that Tom began to consider the offer made by Paul Marinelli and the Barron Collier property. The decision was a difficult one to make, especially after the countless hours he spent designing the campus on the quarry property, but then Tom began thinking about a town designed to support the university and found this idea intriguing. Tom called a few board members to pray about the decision.

The last morning of the extended due diligence deadline, Tom, Nick Healy, and Nick's wife Jane went to Mass at St. Ann's in Naples. The responsorial Psalm at Mass that day was, *"The Lord hears the cry of the poor."* Nick said it felt like a sword went through him as it was read because the Barron Collier property was about eight miles from the small migrant town called Immokalee, which is one of the poorest areas in the state. Nick was convinced that the Scripture that was read in morning Mass was a clear answer to their prayers. His thoughts were: *We are Catholic and belong to the poor.* After Mass they also joined Jack Donahue, a longtime friend of Tom's who had been praying about the decision too. Jack would be the first board member invited on the new board for AMU, and he was the first person Tom talked to when he came to Naples. When Jack first heard of the offer by Barron Collier, he told Tom that he felt the Holy Spirit had inspired it. He thought Tom should seriously consider taking the donated land and save the $125 million land purchase price, which would give him the funds needed to build the university. Now, hearing of Tom's dilemma with the bald eagle spotted on the property he was convinced. Tom began to think that Naples was growing so fast that in a short time it would extend out to the Collier property anyway, so at the last hour he took the Collier deal.

Plans then moved forward to build Ave Maria University on the new site with great resources, tranquil skies, and beautiful sunsets. Because of their location near the small town of Immokalee, AMU students would eventually establish ministries, and children of migrant families would be given scholarships to attend the private K-12 school in Ave Maria and at the university.

As it turns out, they never did see the eagle again. That property is now where The Quarry and Heritage Bay stand today.

JOHN F. DONAHUE, CHAIRMAN FEDERATED INVESTORS INC.: AVE MARIA UNIVERSITY TRUSTEE

I have known Tom Monaghan for 25 years. One morning in early 2002 after 8 am Mass at St Ann's Church, Tom and Nick came over to talk with me and my wife Rhodora about a plan to build a new Catholic university totally faithful to the Magisterium of the Catholic Church. I remembered saying to him that this was a very large and difficult undertaking, but I thought it was a great idea since the so-called "Catholic" universities were not fulfilling what the Magisterium had set forth for Catholic education.

My visits with Tom after Mass became more frequent as he continued to disclose his plans about Ave Maria. On several occasions he came to our home for breakfast, sharing his notes, maps, and drawings with me. One day in mid-April of 2002, he told me that the newspapers had heard of his plan and wanted to interview him. But he had been advised not to meet with the media until he closed the deal on the 2,400-acre parcel of land that he was considering purchasing. I said, "Tom, meet with the newspapers. You don't have much to tell them and they won't write a long article, and then they will leave you alone." All they printed was a short article about his intentions to start a Catholic University near Naples.

However, that article triggered Paul Marinelli to call a friend of mine, Jerry Rauenhorst, who then told me that the Barron Collier Company would give the university 1,000 acres if they would locate the campus on their land near Immokalee. I told Tom about the offer from BCC and said I felt the Holy Spirit had inspired it, so he should seriously consider taking the offer. Tom was very hesitant, because he was deeply committed to the plans for land he had under contract. Also, the new BCC property was 17 miles further inland from his proposed site, and he feared the distance might dissuade students from attending. I remember telling him that if he took the donated land and did not buy the original property, he would save the $125 million land purchase price and then have sufficient funds to build the university himself.

After Mass on the decision day, Tom told me he had been up all night deliberating. I subsequently learned that a bald eagle had been spotted in the middle of the considered property, and it convinced them to not close on that property and to pursue the BCC proposal instead.

What Tom has created with most of his own resources is certainly un-equalled in this country and in the world of higher Catholic education. My admiration for Tom is boundless and my commitment to Ave Maria University is unwavering. I am amazed when I look back at all of the difficult

*challenges that Tom faced in the founding of AMU, and I am truly in awe
to have witnessed his devotion, perseverance, and persistence that allowed
him to conquer each seemingly impossible challenge.*

*When Tom invited me to the AMU Board I agreed to serve for one year
but ended up serving for more than a decade. It has been a great honor
and privilege to have served with him on the board of this outstanding
university, one that for generations to come will serve as the model for
Catholic education.*

On November 20, 2002, officials made their joint media announcement regarding the deal between the Barron Collier Company and Ave
Maria University. The press conference was held in the La Playa Beach
and Golf Club, and the interest was high with a packed room.

They put together a deal with the Barron Collier Company to receive
over 800 acres for the University and to purchase 50 percent interest in
the remaining 10,000, acres with Barron Collier as the general partner
and BCC having responsibility to develop the surrounding town. The
agreement was very complex, so it required a lot of attorney time and
was a very complicated partnership but this freed up Tom to concentrate on the building and the operation of the university. He was concerned that 800 acres might not be enough because so many lakes were
needed to provide the fill since the land had to be raised up five feet because of the high water table. In the end, Tom purchased an additional
100 acres just to make sure the university would have enough land to
grow and expand.

The design would include a town center, or "piazza," which would
border the campus and, in its interior, would be a chapel. Tom knew the
university would need a chapel that would be big enough for both the
students and residents to attend. He was willing to provide the chapel
and shared with Bishop Nevins and Fr. Carosella, the Chancellor for the
Diocese of Venice, his proposal. While the Bishop had no objections,
he suggested using a different name other than "church," but recommended calling it an "oratory" instead. An oratory typically signifies a

house of prayer or chapel, but technically means a structure other than a parish church.

Following the press conference announcing the joint agreement with the Barron Collier Company, a group of those involved met at the Tri Amici Italian Restaurant in Naples and began discussing the design for the new oratory. Tom brought out his notes and, in excitement, everyone added their suggestions as he began sketching an image of what the oratory might look like on the tablecloth, not realizing that it was actually cloth. The owner became aware of this special moment and graciously gave them the tablecloth as a memento of that evening. Jane Healy later had it framed to hang in the Visitors' Center/Museum in the town.

CHAPTER EIGHT

The Vision Becomes a Reality

"For we are co-workers in God's service: you are God's field, God's building. By the grace God has given me, I laid a foundation as a wise builder and someone else is building on it."
1 CORINTHIANS 3: 9-10

When Tom and AMU officials decided to move to Florida, they had to find a temporary campus until the new campus could be completed, and they started by first looking at several struggling hotels in the area. They did finally settle on an unfinished assisted living complex in an upscale residential development in Naples called the Vineyards. The complex had lost its financing and was sitting vacant at the time. Nick Healy began meeting with the developer, Tony Salce, who offered to finish the complex at a donated rate so that students could begin arriving in 2003.

This temporary campus consisted of seven acres and contained two four-story condominium buildings, a resident hall, an indoor-outdoor recreational building, classrooms, offices, library, chapel, and a dining facility. After the first year at the campus, they were able to purchase an adjacent piece of property that included 12 acres and built a library with a central meeting room for events, community lectures, and daily Mass. In addition, they were able to purchase a small nursing home facility next door to use as a male dorm as the student population began to grow. When finished, the temporary campus contained more than 75,000 square feet of available space, enabling them to handle up to 400 to 500 students.

The assumption was that the property would be sold when they moved to the permanent campus, and the proceeds could be used to finance other buildings. Meanwhile, the AMSL Board of Governors was deliberating a possible move of the law school to Florida. While the original plan was to construct a new facility on the same campus as AMU, due to the housing crash of 2008, and a general cash crunch, the board decided to make the move from Ann Arbor to the Vineyards Campus, and rent this campus from AMU.

EUGENE R. MILHIZER: FORMER PRESIDENT, DEAN AND PROFESSOR OF LAW, AVE MARIA SCHOOL OF LAW

When I first became Acting Dean of Ave Maria School of Law, the School's Board of Governors, which Mr. Monaghan chairs, had already made the decision to relocate the law school from Ann Arbor, Michigan to Southwest Florida. I therefore did not participate directly in the decision on whether to relocate the school, but did fully participate in the decision to settle specifically at the Vineyards Campus and, ultimately, in the execution of the relocation decision.

I can say, without hesitation or qualification, that Mr. Monaghan has been an unfailingly committed and generous supporter of Ave Maria School of Law. Indeed, the school would not exist but for Tom's incredible support. More than this, it was Tom's vision in the founding of AMSL and, later, its relocation to Florida, that is most responsible for the school's success. AMSL's first eight years, while located in Ann Arbor, Michigan, were marked by several important achievements. Although the school derived many benefits from its Michigan location, it also was constrained in many ways by its location there. Among these difficulties: AMSL was one of several law schools that were within driving distance of each other, and every other school in the region had a long time—some had generations—to establish connections and relationships there. Besides this, Michigan was the next exporter of attorneys, had a declining population, and suffered economically because of its close ties to the domestic automobile industry.

In contrast, Southwest Florida was by most measures the largest region in the country without a law school before AMSL arrived there. Florida is a net importer of lawyers and has a growing population. Collier and Lee counties have a diverse demographic that is exceptionally well suited for AMSL in that it includes wealthy Catholics and conservatives who can support the school and provide employment for graduates and externship opportunities for students, as well as agricultural workers and others who could benefit from our clinics and pro bono work. Perhaps most importantly, the region has adopted AMSL as its own, which provides us with a strong platform to project nationally and internationally.

Since moving to Florida, AMSL has enjoyed unprecedented success. We have had record enrollment and admissions. We have set new fundraising marks, have attracted first-rate faculty and staff, and we have become financially self-sufficient. We have also retained full accreditation and received acquiescence by the American Bar Association, our accrediting authority, and have built a new and ever-growing base of friends and supporters. The future seems unlimited. All of these more recent accomplishments, just like those in Michigan, can be attributed directly or indirectly to Tom Monaghan's vision and leadership.

Aside from his extraordinary accomplishments, Tom is a good man. He is moral and honest. He has deep religious faith. He is modest and unassuming. He is a visionary and a problem-solver. He is loyal. Although Tom is without question a great entrepreneur and leader, he is an even better person. I will always consider it to be one of the great privileges of my life that I have come to know Tom Monaghan.

On July 1, 2014, it was announced that Dean Kevin Cieply, JD, LLM, would be the third president and dean of Ave Maria School of Law, succeeding President and Dean Eugene R. Milhizer, who announced that he would step down to return to teaching.

"On behalf of the Board of Governors, I take great pleasure in welcoming Dean Cieply as the next President and Dean," said Mr. Monaghan. "Ave Maria School of Law is dedicated to educating lawyers with the finest professional skills and in the traditions of the Catholic faith. Dean Cieply brings with him a wealth of experience that makes him uniquely qualified to guide, inspire, and lead our law school community in our efforts to offer a legal education characterized by the harmony of faith and reason."

Prior to his appointment as the president and dean of Ave Maria School of Law, Dean Cieply served as the Associate Dean for Academic Affairs and Associate Professor at Atlanta's John Marshall Law School. Dean Cieply also served more than 22 years in the Army and Wyoming Army National Guard as a helicopter pilot, Company Commander, and a Judge Advocate General Corps (JAG) Officer. Dean Cieply's last military assignment was as Chief, Legal Operations (Land), North American Aerospace Defense Command (NORAD) and U.S. Northern Command (NORTHCOM), concentrating on counterterrorism and Defense Support of Civilian Authorities. He retired from the military with the rank of Colonel. Dean Cieply is admitted to practice in Arizona, Colorado, Florida, Georgia, and Wyoming, the Ninth and Tenth Circuit Courts of Appeal, and the U.S. Supreme Court.

"I will arrive with an attitude of service; service to our Catholic Mission, to the men and women who work and study at Ave Maria School of Law, to our alumni from both our Naples and Ann Arbor campuses, and finally, service to the community," said Cieply. "I feel extremely blessed to have this opportunity and will treat it as a sacred duty. I literally owe my life to the Catholic Church and its teachings, as it cared for my birth mother during her pregnancy, and arranged for my parents to adopt me. This is my opportunity to give back. And I will give nothing less than my very best each and every day."

In 1998 Ave Maria Institute opened with only a handful of students, and by 2000 Ave Maria College was already a growing campus. In August of 2003 Ave Maria University opened its doors on the interim campus at the Vineyards in Naples, Florida for its first academic year, with 101 students. Students that year represented 33 states from across the country, with 21 from Florida as well as many transfers from Michigan. Before leaving that interim campus four years later, those numbers rose to more than 300 students representing 42 states, as well as 13 countries.

The university offered majors in Biology, Classics and Early Christian Literature, Economics, History, Literature, Mathematics, Music, Political Science, Philosophy, and Theology. (In 2015 the number of majors had increased to 30.) By including two graduate programs in Theology and Exceptional Education it was now able to call itself a university. The most important thing, however, in establishing Ave Maria University was adhering to the bylaws that called for ongoing fidelity to *Ex Corde Ecclesiae*. President Healy did a great job of recruiting and hiring some of the best faculty in the country!

AVE MARIA UNIVERSITY IDENTITY AND MISSION STATEMENT

Founded in fidelity to Christ and His Church in response to the call of Vatican II for greater lay witness in contemporary society, Ave Maria University exists to further teaching, research, and learning at the undergraduate and graduate levels in the abiding tradition of Catholic thought in both national and international settings. The University takes as its mission the sponsorship of a liberal arts education curriculum dedicated, as articulated in the apostolic constitution Ex Corde Ecclesiae, to the advancement of human culture, the promotion of dialogue between faith and reason, the formation of men and women in the intellectual and moral virtues of the Catholic faith, and to the development of professional and pre-professional programs in response to local and societal needs. As an institution committed to Catholic principles, the University recognizes the importance of creating and maintaining an environment in which faith informs the life of the community and takes expression in all its programs. The University recognizes the central and indispensable role of the Ordinary of the Diocese of Venice in promoting and assisting in the preserva-

tion and strengthening of the University's Catholic identity.

It helped that AMU could start from scratch with a blank sheet of paper so that the university was able to avoid many of the pitfalls that other established schools had fallen into, with the most important being to the issue of tenure. They designed the bylaws so that every effort was made to assure that the university remains faithful to the teachings of the Church, in line with the Vatican throughout the generations. Requiring that all Board of Trustee members be committed and knowledgeable Catholics was essential. When it opened, Ave Maria was controlled by a board of trustees of over 20 people, with each one having an equal vote, as well as an advisory board of regents.

The list of honorary degree recipients at AMU looked like a who's who of Catholic heroes. They included, the Most Reverend Carl Mengeling, Most Reverend Raymond Burke, Fr. Frank Pavone, Dr. Thomas Hilgers, Cardinal William Levada, Carl Anderson, Peggy Noonan, and Fr. Richard John Neuhaus, just to name a few. Mother Angelica and Fr. Michael Scanlan were the first recipients to receive that honor from the old campus in Michigan. As the U.S. Bishops stated, "The Catholic community and Catholic institutions should not honor those who act in defiance of our fundamental moral principles." Ave Maria University made that pledge to honor those who bring honor to the Church and never scandalize it by honoring those who do not.

What they were building in Florida was more than mortar and brick. It seemed every aspect of the school, from the building itself to the students, faculty, and board members, was going through a transformation and becoming something new, and there was a shared desire to make what they were doing a success. These were the pioneers, and their confidence, especially during those early days of the university's formation was essential. The most important aspect of the university did not change, however, in the move from Michigan to Florida, and that was its Catholic identity. As a Christ-centered liberal arts-based Catholic institution of higher education, the focus was not just on academics but the development of the whole person, body, mind, and soul. By seeking truth through the light of the Catholic faith, the classroom illuminated every aspect of learning and became an integral part of both the intellectual and spiritual growth of the student. The ultimate goal, then, was for that student to become a light to the rest of society and to wherever their area of learning took them. This is how Ave Maria University was going to have significant impact for saving souls.

REV. MATTHEW L. LAMB: PROFESSOR AND CHAIRMAN OF THEOLOGY AVE MARIA UNIVERSITY, CATHEDRALS OF THE MIND AND HEART

Mr. Thomas Monaghan has dedicated Ave Maria University to the task of fostering Catholic intellectual, moral, and religious life. He often states that the purpose of the university is to provide the best intellectual and faith formation so that her graduates live virtuously in this life and thereby live forever in Heaven. When I spoke with Tom on the need to have M.A. and Ph.D. programs committed to the two millennial great traditions of Catholic wisdom, he saw that the Church and her Magisterium needed well-formed theologians, and so, generously agreed to establish them. President Nicholas Healy, Jr., fully supported the programs, along with the conferences and publications of the Center for Catholic Theological Renewal.

I explained to Tom and Nick that we need Catholic intellectual research, especially in theology as an architectonic wisdom. We need to collaborate, to contribute our small measure, in the building up of what North American cultures, churches, and universities need so desperately: cathedrals of the mind and heart.[1] Cathedrals of the mind, far more enduring than those of stone, wherein we can cultivate attentive reverence

[1] The image came from Fr. Bernard Lonergan, S.J., *Grace and Freedom: Operative Grace in the Thought of St. Thomas Aquinas* (University of Toronto Press, 2000) p. 164. Fr. Lonergan writes of the "vast effort that was needed . . . when the men of Europe emerged from the chaos of a broken empire and the distress of barbaric invasion, and gave their leisure to the construction not only of cathedrals of stone but also the more enduring cathedrals of the mind."

for the goodness and holiness of every real question, of every act of correct understanding and discovery as ultimately gift, a finite created participation in the wondrous, embracing Mystery of the Triune God. We need cathedrals of the mind in which each and every person's restless mind and heart feels at home, in which genuine achievements of every age and every culture and every people will be celebrated in the presence of the Risen Christ.

Our minds and hearts are the very image of God in us, the God who enlightens every human being who ever has, is, and will come into this world, as the prologue to the Gospel of John reveals (John 1:9). We need cathedrals of the mind wherein we can be forgiven by God and one another as we deepen our intellectual, moral, religious reorientations toward truth, goodness, holiness. We need cathedrals of mind and heart in which we can address the massive injustices of history, not with mere moralisms that hurl invectives, but with intellectually and morally sound alternatives that address the shortsighted stupidity which ground the injustice. For justice to flourish, wisdom is needed. To bind up the massive wounds of injustice requires both the compassion of the corporal works of mercy and the enlightenment of the spiritual works of mercy.

Finally, we need cathedrals of the mind wherein we can experience how our own most intimately personal questions, insights, and orientations are intrinsically communal and interpersonal with both the concrete universality of the community of the entire human race and with the Three Persons who are more intimate to each of us than even we are to ourselves. All understanding involves a suffering, a pati, and it is only when the light of our minds is healed and intensified by the light of faith that we can avoid the temptations to cynicism, skepticism, and despairing nihilism when, from all around us and deep within us, come the cries of the victims whom Christ knew and loved as He hung on the cross.

Only with the strength of the Holy Spirit can the extended passion narratives of all of human history narrated in the new covenant be accepted as Gospel, as good news of salvation in the glory of the resurrection. Incorporated within the Paschal Victim are all the victims of history, some of whose stories grace us from the opening pages of Genesis to the last pages of Revelations. They teach us a wisdom that is of God, a wisdom of the Blessed "who have come out of great suffering and been washed in the blood of the Lamb. They shall neither hunger nor thirst nor suffer any more, for God shall wipe away every tear from their eyes." (Revelation 7:14, 17). Only the kenosis of the Divine Wisdom Incarnate in Christ brings good out of evil, grace out of sin, life out of death.

The generosity of Thomas Monaghan has enabled so many to be engaged in the tasks of building such a cathedral of the mind and heart here at Ave Maria University. Long after all the buildings are gone, and the material world as we know it disappeared, the eternally enduring cathedral of all the minds and hearts formed at Ave Maria will be shining in the glory of the Communion of Saints. Deo gratias et Mariae!

To prepare students for this special mission that God was putting on their hearts, Ave Maria University equipped them with a core curriculum in Literature, History, Philosophy, Theology, Mathematics, Language, and Science. Intramural sports, dances, entertainment, service projects, and the opportunity to hear great speakers were among many other activities that were also available on campus or in the nearby communities to round out their university experience and enable them to grow as individuals. On campus there were established "households" where students of the same sex could support one another in their faith. Because of the great number of priests on the faculty, Mass was also offered several times a day to make it convenient for students to attend daily, as well as to receive the sacrament of confession, and priests were often available to assist students in spiritual direction. The adoration chapel that was on campus was likewise regularly used by students and staff alike as they devoted time, individually or with their households, to visit Jesus—and often with their books in tow as they to prepared for a class.

SR. MARY MICAELA HOFFMAN AND SR. MIRIAM MACLEAN: AMU GRADUATES

Sr. Mary Micaela Hoffmann, RSM (Angela Hoffman), and Sr. Miriam MacLean, RSM (Julia MacLean), professed their perpetual vows in the Religious Sisters of Mercy of Alma, Michigan on August 16, 2014. Both are graduates of Ave Maria University. Sr. Mary Micaela received her Master of Arts in Theology in 2006 and Sr. Miriam received her Bachelor of Arts in Theology in 2005.

Sr. Miriam was among the first undergraduates who came to the Naples campus in 2003. She stated that she came to Ave Maria lacking the understanding of her Catholic faith, but it was in her introductory theology class taught by Dr. Riordan that things finally came together for her. It was through that class that she was able to better understand the gift of the Sacraments (especially Confession), apostolic succession, and the freedom and joy that the Gospel brings. Although Sr. Miriam had thought about a religious vocation as a young child, she had put it out of her mind, but it was during this same class and a discussion of Our Lady and her receptivity to the Word of God that she was reminded that she might have a religious vocation!

Sr. Miriam also participated in the first rosary walks at Ave Maria and felt that through them Our Lady was certainly leading her. On one of the first nights after arriving she was invited by other students (Chris Ortega, now Fr. Chris Ortega; John Fischer; Rebbeca Moses) to join them in praying the rosary as they walked around the campus. Not in the habit of praying the rosary, but desirous to see what was happening on campus, she joined them, and then this became a regular part of her nightly routine. These rosary walks have been continued by the students at Ave Maria ever since! That life of prayer that she obtained at Ave Maria laid the foundation for a slow and gradual process of discovering God's will and deepening her life of prayer.

Sr. Mary Micaela was in the first class of graduate theology students at Ave Maria University. She came to Ave Maria after obtaining a Bachelor's degree in Theology from Franciscan University of Steubenville. Her time at Ave Maria became a time of deepening her faith through her studies,

Mass, and personal prayer in the adoration chapel as well as the Liturgy of the Hours. It was also during this time she enjoyed a strong Catholic fellowship with the other graduate students. She had felt drawn to religious life while an undergraduate student, particularly during those times of prayer before the Eucharist; however, it was during her time spent at Ave Maria that she became more certain that this was the vocation to which God was calling her. In God's providence, one of the things that attracted her to the Religious Sisters of Mercy of Alma was their study of St. Thomas Aquinas as part of their formation in religious life, because she had come to love the thought of St. Thomas through her classes at Ave Maria.

Since entering the Sisters of Mercy, Sr. Mary Micaela has spent the last six years in Rome working in service of the Church while continuing her philosophy and theology education. Her studies at Ave Maria provided an excellent foundation for both her religious formation and her studies in Rome. Sr. Miriam spent five years as the Director of Visitor Services at the Basilica of the National Shrine of the Immaculate Conception in Washington, D.C., and earned her Master's degree in Social Work at The Catholic University of America. Sr. Miriam is now Director of Religious Education for the Diocese of Lake Charles in Louisiana.

The fruits of this great foundation that the students were receiving could be seen in two clubs started at AMU, the chastity club and the pro-life club, which were both initiated by the students themselves. Those in the pro-life club took regular trips from the Vineyard campus on Saturdays to Ft. Myers to pray and witness at the abortion clinic there. Currently many of the students go to a Planned Parenthood Clinic in Naples that performs surgical abortions; they go there to minister to those who may be hurting and counsel those who maybe contemplating an abortion. They are also well represented each year at the National March for Life in Washington, D.C., and do many fundraisers for pro-life causes.

On October 18, 2011, a graduate of AMU, Jon Scharfenberger, who was the president of the AMU Students for Life group for many years, succumbed to the injuries he received in an auto accident that also took the life of Students for Life of America Field Director Kortney Blythe Gordon and her unborn child as they were driving back from a conference in Georgia. After graduation (in May 2011), Jon joined the SFLA group as their Campus Support Coordinator, and also become the Pregnant on Campus Coordinator to help train the next generation of pro-life leaders. As president of the SFLA at Ave Maria University, he helped coordinate many fundraisers as well as organizing the prayer vigils at the abortion clinic in Naples. He was a beautiful example to us all and his heroic efforts on behalf of life will always be remembered.

Jon prophetically will be remembered for these words: "You don't know if you're ever going to get there, but you've got to keep following the course. You've got to have faith. You've got to have faith that sometimes is blind, but you just keep holding on and you keep moving forward." Jon followed the course and got to his destination and now AMU has established a pro-life scholarship in his name to help other students find their way.

ANNA SMITH SCARFENBERGER: MOTHER OF JON SCHARFENBERGER

My son Jon was involved in the pro-life ministry throughout his four years at Ave Maria University. It is where he blossomed into a pro-life leader among the youth. While working for Students for Life shortly after graduation in 2011, he was critically injured in a car accident caused by a drunk driver. Ten days later in ICU Jon succumbed to his injuries and died. My boy was 22 years old. It was, however, those ten days of continuous prayers around the nation, indeed the world, that kept me close to God and enabled me to walk this journey. I was reminded that God works out all things for the good of those who love Him.

The Catholic education Jon received at AMU roused in him a thirst for the truth and a hunger for virtue. He learned leadership skills that fostered in him a desire to make a difference in this world. It imbued him with the understanding that the quest of life is to live for God, to get to

Heaven, and while on earth to change the culture of death that pervades our society. Jon worked on his relationship with God; he prayed, all the time, morning, evening, and night prayers. The Rosary was/is his favorite prayer. He even led the people in the Rosary at the Basilica of the Immaculate Conception in Washington, D.C., during the 2010 March for Life. I believe it was at AMU that my beloved Jon was not only educated but formed in Jesus Christ.

Jon received a very special apparition of Our Blessed Mother when he was in Medjugorie in 2009, and now it is she, the Mother of Jesus, who comforts me. I know that he lives with her now and my role as his mother is to continue his legacy in the pro-life ministry by providing funds through the scholarship at Ave Maria University in his name so other pro-life youth can receive an authentic Catholic education and be beacons of light and truth in this ever-increasing dark and secular world.

Since the death of my child I have discovered that love is stronger than death, and this has enabled me to be more sensitive to the whole mysterious process of life and even more trusting in God. Faith teaches us that the fear of death is transformed into hope for eternity, which gives our lives their fullest meaning. Through Jesus Christ death is no longer an abyss of emptiness but rather a path to a life that never ends (John 11:25).

Through the chastity club and the courses taught at AMU, students are better prepared to understand the Church's teachings on the beauty of marriage, and by remaining chaste through those college years are ready and eager to embrace married life upon graduation. They are also open to the gift of children after marriage and many are having large, strong Catholic families who are being taught their faith. In 2014, of the 194 students who graduated from AMU, a record twenty-two couples were engaged, and when you take into consideration those who have already graduated, the stats show that one in five married a classmate.

LILLIAN AND DAN BIELINSKI: MARRIED GRADUATES OF AMU

In ever-increasing ways, I am grateful for my husband, Dan. God has given us the gift of marriage and two beautiful, healthy children, and hopefully more to come! It is with deep joy that I can thank my Lord for these gifts, my marriage, and my family, and it all began at Ave Maria University.

Dan remembers we were in choir together our very first semester, but the basses always sat in the back, and I honestly didn't notice him. After the first drama production on campus, however, I took notice, as did everyone, of this very talented, shy guy. He didn't attend campus social events, but he transformed and lit up the stage. Unfortunately, for the whole year, I thought his name was Tim and wondered why he never returned a friendly greeting!

During our sophomore year, I joined the women's discernment program to seek out my vocation more seriously. This program had a "no dating" policy, which helped me to focus on developing good friendships with both men and women. My friendship with Dan grew especially by being involved in most of the artsy extracurriculars at Ave Maria: plays, musicals, ballet, and cabaret performances. It is a miracle we were able to keep up with our studies! At the time, most of these productions were student-led, which encouraged creative collaboration and backstage camaraderie.

In our junior year, Fr. Fessio asked us to prepare a scene to perform for university fundraising dinners. These "dinners" never panned out, but we thoroughly enjoyed working on a romantic scene together (of Dan's choosing), and considered Fr. Fessio our matchmaker. Dan asked to begin dating, and it wasn't long before we felt marriage was in our future. When I expressed this to my dearest friend, Mary Peterson, I remember her saying: "Go to Jesus, thank Him!" And I hurried to the adoration chapel in our dorm. Truly, "the peace which passeth all understanding" filled my heart, and I praised God and thanked Him for bringing us together.

In our senior year, we performed "I Do! I Do!" This musical has a cast of two, man and wife, and looks at marriage over the span of a lifetime. Although this is an unusual method of pre-Cana, the show brought up all sorts of fruitful conversations about marriage and family life. We were in dress rehearsals for our future vocation!

Throughout these formative years at Ave Maria, we were surrounded by people living their faith passionately: our colleagues, chaplains, faculty, and families of the Ave Maria town community. Classes began with a prayer, and the Catholic faith was taught, respected, and integrated into all the disciplines. There was a positive peer pressure to take advantage of daily Mass, frequent confession, holy hours, and the rosary walks on campus. Every dorm and campus building housed an adoration chapel for immediate and intimate visits with our Eucharistic Lord. Community members were witnesses to the joys of family life and nurturing the domestic church in their homes. This culture of faith and His Presence made all the difference to us as we strove to have a pure relationship and prepare for marriage.

The following years after Ave Maria, we both pursued graduate studies in the arts. Dan studied acting at Columbia University in New York City, and I studied sacred music nearby in Princeton, New Jersey at Westminster Choir College. These were wonderful schools and provided brilliant opportunities. However, the cultural climate change was a bit shocking and disheartening. Without Dan and my formation at Ave Maria, I realize I would have suffered greatly, wondering if there were any Catholic men out there who believed in marriage and practiced their faith. Thanks be to God, our relationship helped us both to remain spiritually steadfast, and our spiritual lives informed our artistic endeavors.

Today we are grateful for our roles as husband and wife, father and mother. Raising our two boys is an immense responsibility that deepens our love and happiness. We live near New York City, relying on each other and trusting God through the ups and downs of an actor's career. God has provided so many unexpected opportunities; we know we are securely held in His hands. Continuing on the path to holiness as a family is our greatest adventure yet!

Having a strong representation of foreign students from many countries is also a great asset at AMU. This is particularly true because there is such a strong student life with all of the students living in dorms. Here they live together, play together, study and pray together, and they learn from each other about the different cultures from all over the world like they never could in class. One of the most important benefits, however, is for the foreign student who is able to receive a degree at Ave Maria to then use their education and formation to make a difference in the world on an international level.

MARUSKA TYSOVA: INTERNATIONAL AVE MARIA STUDENT, CZECH REPUBLIC

My name is Maruška Tylšová, and I come from a small village in the northeastern part of the Czech Republic, where I spent nineteen years before God called me to a wonderful adventure and exciting new life in the United States. My journey began in Prague, after I enrolled as a linguistic student at the University of Southern Bohemia. For it was in Prague that I met a Czech family who asked me if I would like to come to the United States for one year and assist them with their children in Tampa, Florida. I said yes since I always wanted to come to the States to learn English and to better know the culture. Living in a different part of the world with no family or friends was very difficult, but it gave me the greatest opportunity of my life: to seek a close friendship with God.

One day while I was praying in a chapel, shortly before my departure back home, a Filipino girl came in and invited me to a Thanksgiving retreat in Orlando, Florida. It was there that I met students from Ave Maria University. Providentially, I was able to come to Ave Maria the following weekend as my Filipino friend "happened" to be driving there. I remember that as soon as I arrived, I felt like I was in Heaven, as there were friendly and joyful students, Mass three times a day, rosary walks, a beautiful campus, delicious food, and so much more. At that moment, all I wanted was to become an Ave Maria University student so that I could experience the beauty of its Catholic community for more than just one day!

God and our Blessed Mother knew about my desire even more than I did. After my application was accepted and I was awarded an academic scholarship, I began my intellectual journey in this authentically strong Catholic environment. Unlike previous schools, where I encountered mostly value-free theories and intense atheistic biases, I could finally immerse myself in various classes that were true to the doctrine and tradition of the Catholic Church. This experience was absolutely amazing because, having lived in a former Communist country, I had never experienced a community of so many young people, teachers, large families, and people of all ages living the richness and beauty of their Catholic faith. Furthermore, seeing the authentic joy of the students striving to preserve the purity of their bodies and hearts for the love of God confirmed what I have long believed—true fulfillment of the human person is found only in God.

After beginning to take my philosophy and theology classes, many of my questions about God, His plan for creation, the Church, marriage, and family were answered. Thus, I pursued the five-year BA/MA program in Theology so that I could learn more about these truths and share them with others, especially with my family and friends in the Czech Republic. Throughout my studies, I realized that living a spiritually fruitful life is the result of an intimate relationship with God the Father. In this relationship we are called to receive from Him the gifts of creation, Christ, the Holy Spirit, and the Blessed Mother and return ourselves to Him as gifts, which results in the fruits of the Spirit: love, peace, and joy. Such a close relationship with our Father in Heaven is very important because the fruits of love, peace and joy are the best weapons against despair, anxiety, and depression, which are responsible for the culture of death.

This intellectual and spiritual journey gradually led me to an understanding of my vocation to counsel children and adolescents, who have become the main target of psychological and physical abuses of our secularized culture. As a result, I am going to pursue another Master's Degree of Education in Counseling at Providence College. I believe that between my Masters in Theology and a Masters in Counseling, I will be prepared to assist children in finding and experiencing the love of God and to fully explore and cultivate their talents.

When I look back at these five years, I see them as the most fruitful years of my life since I was able to meet many wonderful people with loving and generous hearts, learn about my faith, and find my vocation to serve God through counseling rooted in the Sacred Tradition of the Catholic Church. Most importantly, I came to realize that I have the most loving parents of all parents: my Father and Mother in Heaven, who gave me a second home at Ave Maria. And as I have come to Ave Maria, by Divine Providence, I am leaving Ave Maria, by Divine Providence, for a Providence College in Providence . . . ready for a new adventure. Thank you, my dearest Father and Mother, and all of you who have been helping me on my journey in so many ways.

There was a lot of energy and excitement during those first years at the Vineyard campus in Florida, and the real fruits were being measured in the quality of the students that the university was graduating from AMU. It was rewarding to watch what could happen if students were given the right atmosphere in which to grow their faith.

Father Benedict Groeschel, C.F.R., was an author, preacher, and Servant of the Poor as well as being a former member of the Board of Trustees for AMU and the co-chair of The Cardinal Newman Society's Advisory Board, before his death on October 3, 2014. In *The Newman Guide to Choosing a Catholic College* he stated, "A faithful educational institution is going to prepare people not only for the immediate future of job and career but also for the ultimate future, which is our entrance into the Kingdom of God. A college that does not have this as its top priority does not deserve to call itself Catholic." Ave Maria University is proud to be called a Catholic university and its students are among the very best!

On March 25, 2004, the Feast of the Annunciation, students, staff, faculty, and supporters ventured out to what would become the town of Ave Maria, bordering the Everglades in Eastern Collier County. Under a tent they the celebrated the first Mass before assembling for a special procession of the Eucharist, the Rosary, and a first blessing of the permanent campus and town named in honor of Our Blessed Mother. This feast day has become a tradition that Ave Maria celebrates each year as a sign of gratefulness for all God has done in the midst of the university.

CAROL WEIGOLD: AVE MARIA SEEDS

Carol Weigold is a lady with a green thumb. She loves watching small seeds take root and become plants that can feed and nourish the body. This cycle of life gives her great joy and satisfaction as she, in this small way, becomes united with the Divine. In the spring of 2004, Weigold was visiting a friend in Naples, who invited her on a pilgrimage to the tomato fields that would soon become the town of Ave Maria. She recalls that March day, processing with a large crowd to the place where the Ave Maria Oratory now stands. As far as the eye could see she saw strong green plants, heavy with fruit, and found her own heart heavy with emotion, knowing that all of this would soon come to an end for the new life that was to come.

It was not the loss of the tomato fields that caused her heart to swell but something deeper that affected Weigold, unlike the previous pilgrimages she had made to holy sites throughout the world. She felt she was standing on sacred ground and witnessing a miracle in her midst. At that moment she remembers being struck by the awesomeness of the sacrifice of so many, who, like the plants, were giving up their own personal harvest for a new planting that would carry the seeds of faith and hope into the world.

As Weigold walked through those majestic fields that day, her hands gently brushed the soft fruit, selecting several tomatoes from their vines to carry back to her Greenwich, Connecticut home in the hope of preserving their legacy. Over the past six years she has done just that, carefully maintaining the seeds from the previous year's crop and producing what she proudly refers to as her "Ave Maria tomatoes." Each summer she would generously give her tomatoes to family, friends, and neighbors, sharing with them their origin and how this vision has become a reality.

The seeds now produced in Ave Maria are the students who stand as strong and numerous as those tomatoes once did. They have been encouraged by parents, who have supported their growth, and cultivated by an exceptional faculty and staff who give them root. They find nourishment from those who give generously of their time and treasures to assure that these seeds multiply and produce new fields. In due time they too will become heavy with fruit, and the cycle will continue as they are carried out to feed not only the body but also the soul. This is the miracle of Ave Maria that Weigold felt in her heart that day—and the one that continues to be produced through the fruit of faith.

CHAPTER NINE

From the Vineyards to the Tomato Fields

"I am the true vine, and my Father is the vine grower."
JOHN 15:1

Ave Maria University officially broke ground on February 17, 2006, as Governor Jeb Bush spoke to all those gathered for this momentous event. "This is a historic day, not only for Ave Maria University and town, but also for Collier County and the state of Florida. This new town is the result of many years of work and partnership between state and local government and landowners to develop the Rural Lands Stewardship Program in Eastern Collier County. We thank the leadership of Ave Maria University for choosing Florida as the home for this new world-class academic institution."

As that first shovel hit the ground there were many to be grateful for, including the state and local governments for their involvement in this project, as well as the Barron Collier companies, which were the driving force behind this business venture. There were also many others whose dedication, determination, and hard work made this day a reality. They shared the vision of Ave Maria University from the beginning and were willing to take the risks despite seemingly insurmountable odds.

Looking back on Tom Monaghan's journey, it was hard not to reflect on what had brought him to this moment. Little did he know when he opened that first pizza store to pay his way through college that, forty-five years later, he would be building a university. Similarly, due to the circumstances in his life, he was never able to get past his freshman year in college, but now through Ave Maria University he would be able to give thousands of students the opportunity to receive a first-class Catholic education to go out and really make a difference. He literally started his life in rags, but through hard work and what he would call an amazing amount of luck, he was able to attain what the world perceives as riches. But that day, as he stood there with that shovel in his hand, he was reminded that his money was not his own, but that everything belonged to God. The question, then, is not, *why are we given the opportunities we have* but *what we do with the opportunities that we are given?*

As he thought about those "five priorities" that he pondered while daydreaming as a Marine out in the Pacific, he realized he was right about money. Money is not evil in itself, but the love of money becomes the evil. While he certainly made his mistakes through the years, Tom knew that money could serve a good purpose, and he could think of no greater good than Ave Maria University. He was willing to put everything that he had into building the university, and not just his money but his life. His initial investment had exceeded $300 million, but this would provide only a substantial start. To achieve the vision they would need the financial help and support of others who also believed and would join him on this journey.

In 2004 and 2005 Southwest Florida experienced the worst hurricane season in memory and that, combined with the area's phenomenal growth, second only to Las Vegas, created a big shortage of construction labor and materials. In addition to the problems in Florida, Hurricane Katrina had just devastated New Orleans in 2005, which also impacted building costs. By the time the campus was designed and the university had received all its estimates and bids, the cost had doubled in three years' time.

Zoning was on a fast track, just as the commissioners said it would be. By February 2006 Ave Maria was ready to build Phase I, which included permitting for 11,000 homes and about 1.5 million square feet of commercial buildings—about 5,000 acres for this first phase. The Pulte Company, one of the largest homebuilders in the country, was hired to build about 8,000 of the 11,000 homes, with the remaining homes completed by other developers. In the end the development would have low-income to large estate-sized homes. The county also agreed to widen Oil Well Road, the road connecting Naples to Golden Gate Estates and Ave Maria, and it was completed in 2012. Ave Maria Development needed to put in all the infrastructures, water treatment, wells, roads, and electrical since there was nothing except agricultural land and woods when they first began.

The initial phase of the university consisted of building the Canizaro Library, the Paul Henkels Academic Building, and the Bob Thomas Student Union Building. These benefactors, who acknowledged the importance of this university, the first in the United States to be built in the Catholic tradition in more than 40 years, made significant contributions to the university, and their legacy will always be a part of the history of AMU. Simultaneously the Oratory, Central Utilities Plant, Rhodora J. Donahue Academy (K-12 School), as well as the three dorms, were being built.

The 98,000-square-foot Canizaro Library was named after great supporters of AMU, Joseph and Sue Ellen Canizaro. The library is a state of the art facility that gives students access to all the resources and technology needed to assist them in achieving their goals in any area of study. The library has a seating capacity of more than 400 and houses 200,000 volumes of books that are particularly strong in theology and philosophy, thanks to Tom Loome. It also contains 10,000 volumes of special and rare books that include donations by former U.S. Ambassador Michael Novak from his personal collection and writings, contributions from history and Civil War buff, Carl F. Ellwanger; the collections of AMU Professor, Fr. Matthew Lamb; those of Fr. Peter Milward, S.J, writer and university professor emeritus from Tokyo; former Air Force Major, Daniel Pastor's collections from his world travels; and William

Talbot's large assortment of books, plays, playbills, and reviews that he collected while working as an editor for a theatre publishing company. In addition to those, it also contains the pro-life and pro-family collections of Dr. John C. Willke, the former president of Life Issues Institute, as well as one of the most comprehensive collections on the history of Natural Family Planning that has been compiled since *Humanae Vitae* was released in 1968.

The Paul Henkels Academic Building was dedicated by Paul's family as an appropriate tribute to this man, who was dedicated to education at all levels. Paul was the co-founder of the REACH (Road to Educational Achievement through Choice) program that enabled underprivileged children the opportunity to attend their school of choice, and he, along with his wife, Barbara, co-founded two grammar schools in Pennsylvania, the Regina Coeli Academy and the Regina Angelorum Academy. Paul served as a trustee on the AMU Board from the beginning and as Chairman of the Board from August 2006 until his passing in January 2009. In 2010 the William C. Demetree Auditorium, located in the Academic Building, was also dedicated, posthumously by Demetree's wife, Sara, in honor of this World War II hero and businessman who, among other accomplishments, sold Walt Disney the 12,400 acres of land to develop what is known today as Walt Disney World. His daughter Mary is also a great supporter and member of the Board of Trustees at AMU.

In December of 2008, the Bob Thomas Student Union Building was named to honor Bob, who was known for his generosity and commitment to his Catholic faith. Bob served as the AMU Chairman of the Board from 2004 through 2006 and was instrumental in the development of AMU during the early days. The 63,833-square-foot two-story atrium building is the center of the university's campus life. It contains a chapel, the student dining room, kitchen, and the multipurpose Ballroom (used for large gatherings) on the first floor, as well as a game room, student meeting rooms, and offices on the second. Campus Ministry and Student Life are also located in the Student Union Building. Bob will be remembered as the first chairman of the AMU board and for his deep spiritual approach to problem solving. His willingness to stop a meeting at timely moments and read Scripture or pray, which led to many new solutions and a deep appreciation that God was accompanying the university on this journey.

The dorms were separated into halls for men and women. Sebastian, Goretti, St. Joseph, and Xavier Halls were for men, and the "mega dorms," Mother Teresa and Pope John Paul II, were added in 2009 for the women. Each of the dorms contain a chapel. The dorms are single-sex dorms and not coed. A recreational pool, tennis courts, multi-purpose athletic fields, and the Bowie Kuhn Ballpark, named after Tom's old friend and the former Major League Baseball Commissioner, were added to round out the facilities, all supporting an active student life.

On November 19, 2010 the Golisano Field House was dedicated and named after the co-owner of the Buffalo Sabres, Tom Golisano, whose donation made the Field House possible. Golisano visited Ave Maria three years before and because of the similar backgrounds that he and Tom Monaghan shared, this led to a mutual respect for one another and eventually to Golisano making a major gift for the Field House. The Field House is home to the university's Gyrene sports teams: men's and women basketball, volleyball, and baseball teams; and houses the athletic offices, a training facility, and weight room. The term Gyrene originates from the World War II expression that combines two words, GI and Marine, and communicates discipline, teamwork, self-reliance, and responsibility.

BRIAN TRYMBISKI: 2011 GRADUATE OF AMU AND FORMER RESIDENT DIRECTOR

"I transferred to Ave Maria University in the fall of 2009 from the University of Pittsburgh. I enjoyed my time there on the baseball team, but it was obvious that God had other plans for me after having a season-ending injury, so I decided to try AMU instead. The only reason I chose AMU was due to the indisputable financial benefits that they offered and the opportunity to play ball again.

At first I was reluctant to attend because I was fearful that the Catho-

lic culture at AMU would prove too intense for me, and I perceived the people here as a bit crazy and out of touch with the real world. In the beginning I fought it, but in time I began to notice a big difference in the character of the players on my team compared to those at the University of Pittsburgh, and I grew to really love it. Many of my teammates have since become my best friends that I hope to have for life, but the ability to have Christ as the center of the baseball program turned out to be the best part.

If it wasn't for AMU I don't know where my spiritual life would be. Before I came here I lived a fake spiritual life and did not know the truths of my faith, but since coming here my relationship with God has changed completely. My relationship changed because I was able to get the answers to the questions I had been seeking for many years. Many times in life, Catholics battle the secular world for their faith. The battle involves questions such as: Is God real? Who is Jesus Christ? Why is Mary important? They are bombarded with the questions, but often they do not have the opportunity to look deeper into the truth to discover the answers. At Ave Maria University you are given the opportunity to explore these questions and encouraged to go beyond them to discover who God is and who you are in His greater plan. My view of the Church did not change, but my heart and my relationship with God did. I now have a trust in God in everything that I do.

Choosing AMU allows a student to be challenged academically, grow spiritually, and meet lifelong friends. I feel God is calling our generation to be apostles, sent out to spread His Word and lead by example. AMU equips students to meet that challenge by giving them an outstanding education and knowledge of their Catholic faith. By knowing our faith and receiving the tools to understand the world in which we live, we can spread the Word of God with confidence and intelligence. AMU has literally changed my life!"

The entire campus was inspired by a Frank Lloyd Wright influence, a lot like Domino's Farms, which included large open floor plans and a seamless blending of the exterior and interior design of the buildings, surrounded by open and expansive green spaces. Frank Lloyd Wright commonly used a hip roof, and his favorite roofing material was copper, with wide overhangs. His prairie style architecture had an enduring look, lasts a long time, and looks beautiful as it gets older with its green patina. A few of Ave Maria University's roofs are made of copper thanks to Tom Monaghan's consistent planning for many years to provide the copper that would be needed when the campus actually could be built.

In addition to the buildings themselves, Wright felt there were three important elements that make up beautiful landscaping: water, trees, and hills. The campus had plenty of water because lakes and ponds were formed as the ground was raised to provide the fill for construction, and consequently they were able to put the water wherever they wanted it and in any shape desirable. Trees too were relatively easy to use in landscaping because they were readily available and grow so fast in Florida. However, hills were another story! When Fr. Fessio came from California, he often complained that he missed the mountains and that the only thing that was really elevated in Florida were their bridges. To compensate for the flat contour of Southern Florida, fill was added in a few strategic places to add some contour. Tom's response was, "Two out of three aren't bad!" Visitors often report that the campus is very beautiful.

Starting with a blank slate allowed many to bring their visionary ideas to the table. One employee who had a deep impact on the technology and safety at the campus was Bryan MeHaffey, the initial director of information technology. Bryan was hired when the campus started at the Vineyards, and he had a wealth of experience and connections with many outstanding experts in the growing field of technology. Bryan created a consolidation in the Central Plant that allowed him to combine all the facilities' technologies and IT technologies in a single platform. This was unheard of at the time in most colleges and universities. Most institutions had separate departments managing these areas individually. "What this means is that everything on campus, from the lights illuminating the outside walkways, to the complete phone system, to the building security system and the emails system, all operate through one technology platform. Every system on campus is monitored and managed from one room," Mehaffey said. In 2007 AMU was recognized for its excellence in automation technology by winning the Digie Award (Commercial Real Estate Digital Innovation Award) in the academia division. This annual recognition honors those "who are making the greatest impact through the use of technology and automation." Ave Maria was competing against well-known and established institutions, and that year beat out Carnegie Mellon University and Massachusetts Institute of Technology (MIT). Bryan's creative thinking made this a reality, and in the end his contribution was a tremendous cost-saver for AMU.

The agreement with the Baron Collier Company and Pulte, which was building homes in the town, was that Tom would focus on the university and they would concentrate on the town, with the exception of the Oratory.

As both partners began planning for this 5,000-acre project, it was evident that because of the distance the Ave Maria community was from shopping and amenities in Naples that they were indeed going to be a new town. In their early discussions, the Master Planner suggested using the name Collier. Tom proposed they call it Ave Maria to be consistent with the name of the university. The partners agreed and Ave Maria was born.

Tom kept to his agreement, allowing BCC to do the developing of the town, but did make some important suggestions that were well taken, such as modeling the center of the town as a piazza similar to those that were found in small villages in Italy, and placing the Oratory at its center. Paul Marinelli liked the concept and gave Tom the privilege of naming a few of the streets, such as John Paul II Boulevard, Assisi, Avila, Kolbe, and Annunciation Circle. Tom wanted to keep the various neighborhoods close so they would be in walking distance to the Oratory, but Paul envisioned several neighborhoods within the town itself, more spread out, with their own identities. This concept became a reality.

Initially, six different residential neighborhoods were created: La Piazza, condos above the businesses in the town center; Emerson Park, nearby the private K-12 school; Del Webb, a 55-plus community surrounding a golf course; Bellera, which was later integrated into Del Webb golf community; Middlebrooke, affordable housing that also included graduate accommodations; Hampton Village, with homes surrounding the town center, and in 2012 Maple Ridge and Coquina were also added to the development's expansion.

As word got out about this unique concept, Ave Maria's website was getting so many hits with people inquiring about buying a home in Ave Maria that they expected maybe 450 homes to be built in the first year, with 1,000 units every year after that until it was built out. They were also receiving many inquiries from local and national businesses that were interested in the commercial and retail space that would be available. When the town opened in 2007, the economy had changed, but this space began to fill slowly, with everything from offices to restaurants, an urgent care, a dentist's office, a hair salon, a bank, a university book store, a jewelry store, a women's dress shop, a gift shop, a grocery store, and eventually even a gas station. The pioneering spirit of these business owners in this endeavor was, and is still today, greatly appreciated. Their sacrifices and persistence allowed the locals and visitors alike the same conveniences that a larger town provided.

JEANNE WEBER RUSH: OWNER, THE SECRET INGREDIENT RETAIL STORE, AVE MARIA

My journey to Ave Maria was one of Divine Providence. In the summer of 2004 I was on a buying trip to New York City for my stores, The Secret Ingredient. As I was leaving the hotel for the airport I picked up a copy of the Wall Street Journal *at the front desk, and during my wait at the airport, I began reading an article about the Ave Maria Money Market Mutual Funds that were having some great increases as well as maintaining a strong moral backbone. I spoke to the investor of my IRA and said, "You need to put some of my money in this fund but he could not find it." Then on a Sunday afternoon, August 4, 2004, I decided to search for it on my computer, but instead of finding the Ave Maria Mutual Fund, the town of Ave Maria popped up instead. I was overwhelmed by the beauty of the rendition for the La Piazza shops and immediately emailed the Collier Corporation to inquire about what type of stores they were looking for. I received a quick response on Monday, and the rest is history.*

I have three women's specialty stores in the Midwest, and in the summer of 2006, Rosemary Coyne (a very dear friend of Marge and Tom Monaghan's) walked into my store in Indianapolis, Indiana. After commenting that she lived in Naples, Florida, my sales associate told her that I was opening a store in nearby Ave Maria, and we were immediately connected by phone and have become dear friends ever since. A short time later Rosemary introduced me to Tom Monaghan, and together in 2009 Rosemary and I, along with several other businesses, began the Annual Style Show for Ave Maria University Student Financial Aid, which has been a great success and a lot of fun for those who have attended.

My dad, Dick Weber, and I moved to Ave Maria in December of 2007 and spend our winters there together. Our journey continues in Ave Maria with peace, joy, and very grateful hearts to be a part of Tom Monaghan's vision.

When completed, Ave Maria had a full complement of recreational facilities that included ball fields, a golf course, fitness centers, tennis and basketball complex, and a water park. Residents have access to a dance academy for their children, Montessori pre-school, Theology on Tap meetings, and a variety of other groups, as well as the many university and community events that are hosted throughout the year that draw many visitors and locals into the town. As an unincorporated town, there is no mayor or elected council, but it is run by a governing board and is overseen by the county, for the most part, with a limited power to tax. As the town was being built many people watched it grow from a web cam that was set up on campus as they waited for access to this new town, one that had suddenly generated a lot of curiosity as well as media coverage.

Shortly after Ave Maria opened in 2007 a "perfect storm" hit southwest Florida, and it was not a weather event. The bursting bubble of the housing market and its impact on the stock market made it the worse time in history to build and begin a community. It caused many potential buyers to rethink selling or delay moving, which greatly affected what were initially robust home sales. These sales are now finally recovering, but as Blake Gable, the president of Barron Collier, once said in an interview, "I don't have any concerns at all about where we are. Everything that we did here was taking a look at this community where it sits 50 years from now, not today."

Ave Maria was unlike many other planned communities around the country, especially those newly established in Florida such as the Villages or Celebration City. It was the first modern town in the United States to be developed around a Catholic university with an oratory in its town center. This use of architecture was considered unique and was also met with criticism, but for many centuries churches and towns coexisted together and this was not considered so odd. Tom personally also met with a lot of hostility by the press and other groups who accused him of "imposing his conservative religious ideology on residents," and some even threatened potential lawsuits. Tom believed that people of all faiths and walks of life would be drawn to Ave Maria due to its high moral values in comparison to the rest of the country, and that it was an ideal place to live and to raise a family. "It is our vision that Ave Maria will be a tight-knit, values-based, community-oriented town. It will be a place where individuals, families, students, and retirees of any race, religion, or ethnicity can live and thrive together," Paul Marinelli stated at the groundbreaking ceremony. "It will truly be a real hometown for its residents." This statement is a true reflection of those who live in Ave Maria and why, in recent years, many more residents and businesses are being drawn here.

AVE MARIA RESIDENT, JOHN DEFELICE: DISCOVERING CHARLES

One day, while spending the winter of 2010 in Ave Maria, my wife Patti mentioned that she had been with a neighbor of ours in Del Webb, Peggy Stinnet, who shared something very interesting with her. She mentioned that her daughter-in-law Katie, who lives in Michigan, had recently been to a DeFelice family reunion in Youngstown, Ohio and wondered if there might be some connection with our family. I knew my Uncle Tony and Aunt Carmel lived in Youngstown, but I was unsure of the possible connection with Katie, so when I returned home to York, Pennsylvania, I looked at our De Felice family tree and found out that Katie was the granddaughter of my first cousin Charles! Charles Testa was the son of my father's oldest sister, Colletta, and although all of the other siblings had settled close to New Castle, Pennsylvania, when Aunt Colletta married she had moved to Michigan. The extended family would get together quite often, but my memory was when Aunt Colletta would visit she would often come by herself, and although I knew that she had a son named Charles, I had no memory of ever meeting him.

After confirming that Katie's grandfather, who they called "Charlie," was indeed my first cousin, Peggy agreed to have them down to Ave Maria when her daughter-in-law was visiting so we could all get together. I of course wanted this to be a very Italian reunion with great food and fellowship, to which my wife Patti agreed.

When the date was set, I was like a kid anticipating Christmas! I was about to meet a cousin, who was about 80 years old, for the very first time! We met Charles and his wife Norma on a Sunday just before Mass, and I got the feeling that he was as excited about the reunion as I was. Our meeting brought back a flood of pleasant memories of things that I haven't thought about for years. During Mass, as I sat next to Charles, I thanked God for allowing me to make this family connection. In Ave Maria we have learned that there are no such things as coincidences, because where God is involved, miracles exist. I think all of our relatives were smiling down at us that day!

As this new town and university began to take form, one could only think of the mile long rows of tomatoes and peppers that once covered these grounds. Tomatoes that were possibly used to make the pizzas that were now delivering opportunities to produce the miracles that would continue far into the future.

CHAPTER TEN

The Ave Maria Oratory

"For every house is built by someone,
but the builder of all things is God."
HEBREWS 3:4

The partners estimated that Ave Maria would have many committed Catholics living in town, as well as visitors and students attending Mass, and that Ave Maria was going to need a big church. The original plan was to build an oratory that would seat 3,300 people and stand 185 feet tell, all at the estimated cost of $37 million. However, everyone was shocked when the prices continued to increase and final figures came in close to $80 million. The only solution was to simply downsize. The final plan ended up bringing the seating capacity down to 1,100, with a height of 104 feet, and a total of 27,000 square feet. However, due to the increased costs associated with the construction of the university, even those adjustments came in at a price that were excessive.

To save money the administration decided to make even further cuts, but both Collier County and Pulte agreed that it was important to the community that the Oratory retain its size. Since the Oratory was to become the centerpiece of the town and the logo of the campus, as well as signifying the importance of the spiritual dimension of AMU, the decision was made to stick with the plan and wait on some of the non-essential interior and exterior work until donations could be solicited to complete them. Tom was very hands-on in the design at almost every level and directed the architect, Harry Warren, from Cannon Design.

The cornerstone of the Oratory was laid on the Feast of the Annunciation, March 25, 2006. Architect David Uppgren, who designed Tom's home in Ann Arbor and did the build-out of Domino's Farms, recommended Cannon Design. Based in Grand Island, N.Y., the staff at Cannon worked on the restoration of Frank Lloyd Wright's Martin House in Buffalo. Many believed that the Oratory design was based on the shape of a bishop's miter, but the truth is the design was based on Fay Jones' chapels. Jones, a student of Frank Lloyd Wright, was one of America's most admired architects, especially by other architects, and he received special recognition for the beautiful chapels he built, primarily around his home of Fayetteville, Arkansas. Thorncrown was one of those chapels inspired by the great cathedrals of Europe. It was built in Eureka Springs in 1980 for $158,000 on a private piece of property in the woods of Northwest Arkansas. It's been said that its picture was published more than any other architectural masterpiece in the '80s.

Tom knew Fay Jones because Jones was building a house for him in Ann Arbor in the '80s, just before he took his "millionaire's vow of poverty," and he also built Sam Walton's home. Jones was the most renowned of all Wright's students. In 1990 Fay Jones won the coveted Gold Medal in architecture; he died in 2004. He is recognized as one of the top ten architects of the 20th century. In planning the Oratory at Ave Maria, Tom simply took ideas from a number of Jones' chapels, including Thorncrown and the Mildred B. Cooper chapel in Bella Vista, Arkansas, and expanded them into a much larger building. Using the same concept, the design used steel to create an open lacing of arches that were both structurally integral to the building itself but also gave it a spiritual dimension and beauty. At its completion Cives Steel, of Thomasville, Ga., used 1,270 tons of fabricated steel on the project. Thorncrown and Mildred B. Cooper were both covered with glass that allowed in the natural light, but in Florida Tom knew that would not be feasible with the potential of hurricanes, so he chose aluminum for the Oratory roof instead. Skylights were added along the exterior beams and the roof ridge to offer the continuous lighting needed as well as the natural light from the Rose Window on the facade and dome over the altar. Inside, chandeliers were created, using a Frank Lloyd Wright concept that replicated the ones used in Sam Walton's home. Each one is 11 feet tall, weighs 800 pounds, and carries 504 watts of electricity.

The design of the Oratory interfaced stone with steel, giving it a design that had some modern elements to it but allowed it to still kept the gothic feel of the European basilicas. On the exterior fascia a "travertine stone" was brought in from four different quarries in New Mexico, and a smooth cast stone, or "facing stones," were used on the outside and inside walls that became naming opportunities for donors. In fact, throughout the Oratory you will see the names of those who in the months and years following the construction donated holy water fonts, pews, confessionals, brick pavers, and more, with just about everything being gifted from the generosity of those who believed in the mission of Ave Maria and who have now joined the 60,000 other individuals who proudly call themselves our Founders.

Tom's idea of the Founders began in 2002 to help establish the funds needed for the university to grow. Most established universities have the support of alumni and endowments to aide them in expanding or adding programs, of which AMU had neither, but what it did have were fellow Catholics who were aware of the crisis the Church was facing and wanted to do something about it. As the number of Founders grew, clubs began to spring up in different parts of the country that used the same model as Legatus. Founders meetings were open to everyone and included Mass, a meal, speaker, and updates on AMU. They were like small franchises as information about both the university and community's progress was shared. These Founders were similar to stockholders in a company, but their investment was to reap a great harvest of souls!

Fr. Fessio, who was the Provost of Ave Maria University, had a plan to reach out to these Catholics through a mass mailing and share with them this promising endeavor, as well as to offer them an affordable means to become a Founder through a minimum donation of only $10 per month. Within a short period of time thousands of responses began to pour in from all over the country as 25,000 Founders quickly became part of this historic initiative. These "cloud of witnesses" pledged gifts large and small but also supported the university with their prayers. They became "alumni in faith".

Some donations came miraculously, and many had their own story to tell. The tabernacle, which is the main focus of the sanctuary, was designed by Tom and built by an artist in Spain. The tabernacle was donated by Elizabeth Romeo, who wanted to remember her late husband in a beautiful and profound way. Shaped in the image of the Oratory, it is covered with blue enamel and trimmed in gold and there are thirteen tanzanite gem stones located on the facade, with each valued greater than a 3.5-carat diamond. Adorned on each side of the tabernacle are gold-gilded angels.

DR. CAROLE CARPENTER: FORMER VICE PRESIDENT OF UNIVERSITY RELATIONS (2000- 2011)

It was our first day at the new campus and we were all so happy to finally have a permanent home. Liz Romeo came to visit the campus that day to make a donation. Everyone knows how hard it is to move with a family of three or four, let alone a family of over 200 people. We couldn't find our brochures, the computers weren't working, and we were surrounded with boxes. As I looked for my desk chair, I received a call from the visitor's center letting me know that a woman was there and she was asking for me to discuss a gift. When I got there she said, "Don't talk me into anything; I know what I want. I want a pew in memory of my dear, late husband, Anthony."

I knew that all the pews had been donated, and so I told her that we could not offer a naming opportunity for a pew. She wanted to know what was left. Jack Rook found his laptop and we showed her a DVD showing a rendition of what the Oratory might look like when it was finished. When

Liz saw the tabernacle she was overwhelmed and asked, "What about the tabernacle?" I gently indicated that the donation for the tabernacle was many times more than the donation for a pew. I suggested the Stations of the Cross, the confessionals, or things of that nature. She asked again about the tabernacle, and I shared with her the size of the gift that would be needed. She said, "Oh no, let's look at the film again." Once more we watched as she was drawn to the tabernacle. I asked her if she would consider making the gift over five years and she seemed upset with me. When she had said that she did not want to be talked into anything, I felt that I might have crossed a line with her. Then suddenly she answered, "Why would I do that?" and she opened her heart and her purse to write a check for the tabernacle. I think we were both in awe in that moment at the significance of the gift.

That day as I was driving home, I was struck by the fact that all day long everyone had been expressing the sentiment that we finally had a home. We had previously been in an elementary school in Ypsilanti, Michigan and then at a temporary campus in Naples at the Vineyard's. As the years passed we would make annual visits to the tomato fields on the Feast of the Annunciation. Praying and believing that we would someday have a permanent campus that would be our home.

Now on the first day that we occupied the new campus, God sent a Founder to ensure that He would have a home in our midst. This was the first major gift to Ave Maria University on the new campus and a permanent reminder that He is with us and accompanying us in this journey.

Slowly the interior of the Oratory began to take shape, and over the weeks and months ahead the excitement began to build as more donations were received and new additions to the Oratory took their proper place. The crucifix (Latin *cruci fixus,* meaning "fixed to a cross") that hangs over the altar was generously donated by Glory and Tom Sullivan, but upon its arrival in February of 2009 its installation became an engineering challenge.

The crucifix contains a 23.8-foot-tall red oak cross that weights 2,600 pounds, and a cast bronze corpus that is 12.7 feet tall, weighing 1,600 pounds; the corpus was sculpted by Canadian artist Timothy Schmalz. When the crucifix arrived, the corpus and cross needed to be separated to fit through the Oratory doors, and even after being detached, the corpus only cleared them by 1/16" of an inch!

It took a week, and many men, to build the scaffolding that was necessary to raise and hang the crucifix, with its combined weight of 4,200 pounds. Those who watched its progress said it felt like they were watching the Roman soldiers raise the cross at the crucifixion. Unintentionally, after its installation, an amazing view of the crucifix unfolded. During certain times of the day when natural lighting comes through the Oratory, the lighting that is displaced creates a shadow on either side of the cross resembling the two thieves that hung with Jesus during the crucifixion! Another interpretation one priest gave was that it is "symbolic of the Trinity." Visitors and those who worship in the Oratory find this to be a very special spiritual experience, one that speaks to each individual in a different way.

The interior statues of the apostles over the altar are made with Linden Wood from Czechoslovakia. The statues weigh, on average, between 218-289 lbs. and stand approximately 6 feet tall. From left to right are: St. Peter, St. Andrew, St. James the Less, St. John, St. Phillip, St. Bartholomew, St. Thomas, St. Matthew, St. James, St. Jude, St. Simon, and St. Matthias. The larger statues of Mary and Joseph also have their special places in the sanctuary and were donated by special donors from St. Louis, Joseph and Rosemary Shaughnessy.

The Stations of the Cross were donated and restored by Tony and Suzanne Rea, from Michigan, who found them in the basement of St. Agnes Church in Detroit the day before the church was to be demolished. Through a series of artistic representations, often sculptural, the 14 stations take you on a spiritual pilgrimage from when Jesus was condemned to death to being laid in the tomb. Each of the stations found in the Ave Maria Oratory is a 90-year-old, bas-relief format (three-dimensional sculpture) that was created using the Scagliola means, containing a mixture of plaster and marble. The amazing thing was that the frames for the stations were already built before they received the donation, but they fit perfectly!

The Stations of the Cross border the interior walls of the Oratory as do the eight confessionals that are an important part of the sacramental life of the Church and used often by the students and town people in Ave Maria. The Sacrament of Reconciliation is one of the most unique and beautiful aspects of Catholicism as Jesus Christ, in His abundant love and mercy, established the Sacrament of Confession so that we as sinners can obtain forgiveness for our sins and are reconciled with God. *"Jesus said to them again, 'Peace be with you. As the Father has sent me, even so I send you.' And when he had said this, he breathed on them, and said to them, 'Receive the Holy Spirit. If you forgive the sins of any, they are forgiven; if you retain the sins of any, they are retained'"* (John 20:21-23). As one's faith is nurtured and grows, the need for this sacrament takes on greater importance, and while its practice has diminished over the years, it is coming back strong. Visitors comment that it is a joy to see so many people taking part in the Sacrament of Reconciliation. As they say, "build it and they will come." God knows what He's doing.

The fifty-four pew ends that can be seen throughout the Oratory are engraved with the names of many benefactors and were designed by David Uppgren and Tom Monaghan in the Frank Lloyd Wright style. They were finished in Ann Arbor by a group of volunteers from Domino's Farms that have warmly been named the "pew crew." Each pew was prayerfully donated by families that supported Ave Maria before the Oratory was finished. In fact, there is a wall in the library that also bears the names of these donors, along with 20,000 others who gave gifts to support the founding of Ave Maria even before the move to the new campus. The tile floors throughout the Oratory were made using a Brazilian slate tile called ardosia that, through time, has developed its own unique color and pattern.

Flanking each side of the outside large Oratory doors are the statues of Our Lady of Guadalupe and the Infant of Prague, which stand 66 inches tall and are made out of Ghibi granite obtained from a quarry in

India. On the north side of the Oratory entrance is the sculpture of Our Lady of Guadalupe, donated by Angie and Jack Giambalvo from York, Pennsylvania. Our Lady of Guadalupe is the "Patroness of the Americas" and one of Mexico's most popular religious and cultural images. This representation of Our Lady is also widely used as a strong prolife symbol as she appears pregnant, carrying the Son of God in her womb. Living so near the migrant town of Immokalee it is fitting that this Hispanic representation of Our Lady has a special place here.

In the adjacent niche stands a depiction of the Infant of Prague that was donated by Bob and Penny O'Brien, Bill and Susan McIntyre, and Tom and his wife Marge. It is an image that was created by a Spanish monk who received a vision from the Christ Child. The Infant is portrayed holding a miniature globe in his left hand, surmounted by a cross, signifying the worldwide kingship of Christ. The right hand is extended in a blessing with the first two fingers upright to symbolize the two natures in Christ, while the folded thumb and last two fingers touch, representing the mystery of the Holy Trinity. The image was brought to the city of Prague in 1628 and, after many battles, it was later discovered damaged in the ruins of a church by a faithful priest who heard the Infant Jesus say, "The more you honor Me, the more I will bless you." The statue was later restored with many miracles and worldwide devotion attributed to it. The Infant of Prague is known to be the patron of universities, vocations, family life, and travelers, to name a few, which pretty much encompasses everyone who lives and visits Ave Maria.

Located between the sculptures and standing guard over the threshold to the Oratory in the exterior niches are the twelve apostles. The gilded gold statues stand 36 inches tall and are a reminder to us of the gift of faith that we have received that began with these twelve ordinary men whose lives were transformed into saints.

In 2008 world-renowned Hungarian sculptor Marton Varo was chosen to create the primary facade of the Annunciation as the focal point of the Oratory's main entrance. The depiction of the Annunciation was chosen as a symbolic work to honor those words first spoken to Mary, and on whom this university is named, *"Ave Maria,"* which is Latin for Hail Mary. This was the salutation the Archangel Gabriel used at the Annunciation when he announced to Mary that with her consent she would become the Mother of Jesus. The sculpture is 35 feet tall and 31 feet wide and composed of fifteen pieces of marble that weighed 120 tons before its carving and 54 tons at its completion. The relief of the Blessed Mother itself is 20 feet tall and is now one of the largest depictions of Mary in the world. The Carrara marble that was used for this sculpture came from the quarry, Cave Michelangelo, at the foot of the Apuan Alps in Tuscany, which was also the source for the flawless white marble used by Michelangelo's *David* and the *Pieta*. The project was underwritten by Michael Windfelt.

Marton Varo became a familiar site on the grounds of Ave Maria for almost three years as he worked on the sculpture in full view, before leaving in May of 2011 at its completion. The final relief was dedicated and unveiled on the Feast of the Annunciation on March 25, 2011 to a crowd of thousands.

MARTON VARO: SCULPTOR OF THE ANNUNCIATION OF MARY RELIEF

I have devoted my life for the last three years to the project. This has probably been the happiest time of my career, and I couldn't wait to start work each day. It was a good feeling to know that I was welcomed, supported, and my work appreciated.

Putting these pieces, fifteen of them, up on the front wall of the Oratory was a real technical challenge; however, it was not due to the weight but because of the niche situation. We needed to reach inside that area to place each piece, and the crane couldn't do that. Luckily, we had Skip Doyle, a wonderful friend, fan, and very good engineer, who not only designed, but had the manufacturer, Salazar's Shop in Immokalee, do everything immediately for us. An enormous cantilever was manufactured in a matter of two days, so we were able to continue to put up those heavy sections, some of them weighing about seven tons. Mr. Edward Jackoboice

gathered his friends and former business partners to also assist us, and
Mr. Roger Betten helped us to find the crane.

It took 150 cement trucks to set the foundation for the Oratory and 17 hours for it to be poured, making it the longest concrete pour in Florida's history: 3,000 yards of concrete, 3 feet thick. Its final dimensions were 27,000 square feet and 206 feet long, and the final building cost was $34 million. In 2008 the Ave Maria Oratory won the TCA Achievement Award as well as an award from the American Institute of Steel Construction.

On July 27, 1984 Bishop John Joseph Nevins was appointed the first Bishop for the Diocese of Venice as portions of the Archdiocese of Miami and those of Orlando and St. Petersburg were divided to create this new diocese due to the tremendous growth that had taken place in south Florida. On January 19, 2007, less than a year after breaking ground in Ave Maria, Archbishop Pietro Sambi, the Apostolic Nuncio to the United States, made the announcement that he had accepted Bishop Nevins' resignation at the age of 75. Archbishop Pietro Sambi also announced that the Coadjutor Bishop of Venice, Most Reverend Frank J. Dewane, would be installed in Bishop Nevins' place. Early on, when Tom Monaghan and President Healy met with Bishop Nevins about being a parish, they were told there would be some advantages to being a parish, but the university also, needed a student chapel, so it was a unique situation.

While they were waiting for the Oratory to be completed, the university was given permission by Bishop Dewane to say Mass in the Student Union Ballroom on campus. In November 2007 the Oratory was completed, and Bishop Dewane made the decision that due to the number of families and individuals that lived in the community who would need the Sacraments over the coming years, that the Oratory should become part of a diocesan plan for the spiritual needs of the Ave Maria Community. The term "Quasi Parish" was then used to define this unique arrangement. As a "Quasi Parish" Ave Maria could exist as a parish in the diocese to provide the sacramental life that the university and the community required until such time that the community grew and could build a new church with proper offices, meeting rooms, and a parish center.

On March 31, 2008 (the celebrated feast day of the Annunciation because March 25th fell during Easter Week that year), Bishop Frank Dewane dedicated the Oratory and celebrated its inaugural Mass as the faithful participated from inside the Oratory and satellite locations around the campus because of the large crowds who attended. Following the dedication prayers, sacred Chrism oil was used to bless the Oratory walls marking the north, south, east, and west corners of the building and dedicating it as a house of worship. Sacred oil was then used to bless the altar where the Holy Eucharist was celebrated in the Oratory for the first time. Near the end of the dedication it was announced that the diocese had appointed Fr. Robert Tatman as the priest administrator of the new Quasi Parish of Ave Maria, a title that in time would be changed to pastor. In 2013 Fr. Cory Mayer would become the second pastor of the Ave Maria Oratory.

When Tom was asked later by a reporter "who is in charge," he pointed to Bishop Dewane. Tom told him, "We respect the bishop, we're always obedient to the bishop, and we've always intended to be. If we don't do that, we're hypocrites as far as being a Catholic university. That's the way the Church is structured, and that's the way I believe it should be."

When the Oratory was finally dedicated and blessed, what was once just a building became the dwelling place of Christ with Jesus now residing permanently in the Tabernacle. In those early days more than 50,000 visitors were coming to Ave Maria a year. Some had never entered a Catholic church before in their lives. Maybe it was the curiosity of the town and Oratory that drew them, but many who came expressed to the students who greeted them as they entered the Oratory that they felt a presence there that was hard to describe. Still, today, this place is bringing many back to their faith as people from all walks of life and many nations visit and stop to say a prayer or attend a Mass at the Oratory.

In 2009, with the Bishop's blessing, Ave Maria University opened the Martha J. Burke Chapel adjacent to the Oratory, where perpetual Eucharistic Adoration became available for students, the community, and visitors to spend time with the true presence of Our Lord in prayer. Christ instituted the Holy Sacrament of the Eucharistic to remain with mankind until the end of time (John 14:18) and the students and the community retain a 24-hour presence here as they silently wait and watch with Jesus (Matthew 26:40) in this small chapel. Christ's presence and special graces are available to all who visit and seek to draw nearer to Jesus through this special devotion.

Carole Carpenter, the former director of university relations at AMU, said that after moving to the new campus Tom Monaghan would continually ask at their Monday administration meetings when the Adoration Chapel would be opened. This was of utmost importance to him as Adoration was a vital part of the previous campuses, and because most religious communities have that spiritual mantle over them to assist them in succeeding in their mission.

At first the plan was to have the Adoration Chapel in the Student Union Building, which had a lovely chapel and access would be allowed to those in the community. After many months of prayer, however, the Bishop wisely recommended that it be located at the front of the library, where the public could participate more fully and the community could help cover the hours of Adoration more easily. Because of this change in plan, the university was then met with the challenge of having to redesign this space, get permitting, and reconfigure what was once an exit door to the library into an Adoration Chapel. The final cost was $250,000.

Dr. Carpenter said that shortly after receiving those figures she went back to her office and received a call from one of the university's major donors. The donor shared with her that she had spoken to another Founder who asked if there was a need for the Adoration Chapel. He said that his mother-in-law, Mrs. Martha Burke, was critically ill with cancer and that he wanted to make a donation in her name. When Dr. Carpenter asked how much the donor was thinking of giving for this project, he said, "$250,000!"

To everyone's sadness, Mrs. Burke never did get to see the chapel. On the day of the dedication she was scheduled to fly to Ave Maria on a medical plane to be there, but there was a shuttle launch that day and the private plane was grounded. On the day of the dedication Fr. Robert Garrity (AMU Director of Campus Ministry) said, "We are extremely grateful to the donor for contributing the funds necessary to create this beautiful chapel and providing a place of prayer and meditation for members of AMU and the surrounding community." Shortly afterward the university received word that Mrs. Burke had passed away.

Dr. Carpenter said that each time she goes into the chapel and sees Martha Burke's name on the door, she says a prayer for her and asks her to pray for Ave Maria. She thinks Martha would be very pleased to see so many students, visitors, faculty, staff, priests, and town people spending time with Our Lord in this very special way. Yet another story of grace and guidance, as God blessed the beginnings of Ave Maria, and continues to do so.

FATHER ROBERT GARRITY: AVE MARIA UNIVERSITY'S DIRECTOR OF CAMPUS MINISTRY

I consider myself to be extraordinarily blessed and privileged to serve as Ave Maria University's Director of Campus Ministry and to work with and for Tom Monaghan. When a deeply faith-filled Catholic man urges a priest to make a positive difference in the spiritual lives of students, it can make the priest's life very gratifying and the students' lives truly worth living. I would like to mention just a few thoughts on Tom's hopes for the spiritual lives of Ave Maria students, but I must inject that it is his greater vision to excellence in education in the Catholic tradition that has and will continue to have this same impact on others outside of the university and far into the future.

For years Tom Monaghan wanted, desired, and longed for a perpetual Adoration Chapel on the AMU campus. Being a humble and generally patient man he never directly told me his deep sense of urgency about this until one day in 2009, when he said, "I want a perpetual Adoration Chapel on campus, where the Lord can be adored seven days a week, twenty-four hours a day," and knowing this, I said, "Yes, we will make that happen." With God's grace and the generous donation of a benefactor in a very short period of time, we were able to open the Martha J. Burke Adoration Chapel. Tom himself did not just "talk the talk" about the Adoration Chapel but immediately "walked the walk" by filling in the 1 a.m. time slot even though he gets up at 3:45 a.m. every day! Since that time many countless blessings have come to us through the Adoration Chapel, blessings of both a spiritual and material nature.

Abundant blessings have also been attained through Tom's encouragement for having Marian devotions on campus, the nightly Rosary walk by the students, and special processions on major feast days. We have been powerfully graced by these events and our students have certainly benefited from them in many ways.

Tom is also excellent in what I would call the field of "practical" theology and has a simple, straightforward way of living his own Catholic faith and helping others do the same. He is thoroughly convinced that a strong spiritual life and a high intellectual life go hand in hand. In other words, you would be able to think better if you prayed better and would pray more effectively if you thought more clearly about God and your place in the universe. Tom would often ask me if it was true that a person in the state of mortal sin would be unable to function as well as that same person who was in the state of grace, and I always told him, "Yes, that's true." Then Tom would remind me to urge our students to stay in the state of grace, because their lives would be far better in every way than if they were in the state of mortal sin, to which I would reply: "Amen."

I also heard Tom on several occasions state that his deepest desire for our students was for them to attend Mass every Sunday (and every day, if possible) as well as pray the Rosary every day. How many billionaires do you hear saying that to young people? Not many, sad to say. Tom's recipe for happiness and success was very simple and direct: pray hard and think well. I have personally witnessed the fruits of this winning philosophy, especially in the dining hall, where I often hear these faith-filled students in dinner conversations discussing serious intellectual topics ranging from metaphysics to pro-life service, a rare group of subjects in today's superficial world.

Reflecting upon the day-to-day spiritual lives of the students at Ave Maria University, what we try to do through the Department of Campus Ministry, along with Student Life, is to make available to our students the riches of the spiritual life, especially those blessings which flow from the Catholic Faith and culture. Students are invited and encouraged to get involved in activities that enrich their spiritual lives, namely, everything from adoration and spiritual direction to on-campus clubs and off-campus service projects. Yet there is never any pressure or coercion. If a student chooses to avoid any involvement in spiritual events, that is respected. We propose; we do not impose.

Recently Tom was very proud when a major journal of thought named Ave Maria University as the "Most Catholic University in America." Tom took this as an affirmation that the university was moving in the right direction, although we are still young and have a lot of growing to do. He always wanted Ave Maria University to be a spiritual powerhouse, which it has become, and will be even more so in the future, with God's help.

All of this is because a humble and holy man who wanted to give back has made a tremendous impact for the good by founding this outstanding university to help students grow in knowledge and their Catholic faith. It can be said that the benefits of doing so are literally out of this world!

CHAPTER ELEVEN

City on a Hill

"You are the light of the world. A city set on a hill cannot be hidden."
MATTHEW 5:14

When traveling to Ave Maria, long before you reach the town itself, you can see the Oratory in the distance. Years ago ship captains used to look for markers like this to identify cities, and it was said that the tallest building in a town signified its importance. In the past it was always a church that held this place of distinction, but today, sad to say, skyscrapers now tower over them instead.

Puritan John Winthrop referred to America in its early history as that "city on a hill," referring to it as a place where "the eyes of all the people are upon us," and this was also a phrase used by past presidents such as John Kennedy and Ronald Reagan. This analogy is not unlike a Scripture found in Matthew 5:14, where Jesus said, *"You are the light of the world. A city set on a hill cannot be hidden."* The "eyes of all the people" were upon Ave Maria, especially during those first years.

Most of us grew up in neighborhoods where children could play outside, freely ride their bikes, walk to the candy store, and attend sporting events together. Ave Maria was very much like that as it began to grow and attract individuals who wanted those same values restored. The story of the town's growth was slow in the beginning due to the economic crisis, but in some ways this promoted the deep community spirit that became Ave Maria's foundation and "brand of living." There were many others who showed interest and wanted to move here as well but found difficulty in selling their homes in other parts of the country. In time, however, they too were able call Ave Maria their home.

With the university in operation, the private K-12 school up, and the surrounding neighborhoods growing, the community became a multi-generational village like many of the small towns in America. Soon businesses began to open that included a bookstore, coffee shop, woman's boutique, jewelry store, hair salon, a dentist, urgent care, a gift shop, dance studio, and a UPS store. In town faculty could often be spotted having discussions with their students over coffee, neighbors met for dinner, and Mass was celebrated often in the Oratory for the benefit of both the students and the residents.

As Ave Maria celebrated its tenth year in operation, 700 homes had been sold, and those numbers are changing daily. It has an online newspaper, *The Ave Herald*, a Publix grocery store, a pub, bank, organic farm, gas station, pizzeria, Tropical Smoothie, a chiropractor, realtor, as well as many other offices and businesses. People of all ages and nationalities live here and many faiths and political views are represented. It is not a community without challenges, but is a place where neighbors care for neighbors, education is valued, and good friends live closer. Also, with the growth of conferences and outside speakers as well as invitations from the university to plays and musical performances, it is fun place to live.

In the center of the town stands the Oratory with its 13-foot Celtic cross on top, donated by Dian Jennings Mayo. The circular design is a representation of God's unending circle of love and mercy. In the evening you will often see an owl perched there; this magnificent creature seems to have made it his job to look out for Ave Maria and his presence is also symbolic of a popular prayer that is often spoken here: *"Our*

Lady Seat of Wisdom . . . pray for us!" The cross is a magnificent symbol of God's presence in this community.

THE LAST GIFT: THE SONNY RUBERTO STORY

Sonny (John) Ruberto was a major league baseball player who played for the San Diego Padres, the Cincinnati Reds, and was first base coach for the St. Louis Cardinals. In his early baseball career he was mentored by the legendary Sparky Anderson when he was with the St. Louis Cardinals organization. Sonny met his wife, Karen, on Friday, October 13, 1961, the Feast of Our Lady of Fatima, and they married right after high school as Sonny began traveling for his baseball career. Years later at the age of 29, after starting a family, it was discovered that Sonny had kidney disease, something that would be a lifelong cross but also bring both he and Karen into a deeper conversion of faith.

In March of 1984 Sonny attended the Christ Renews His Parish (CHRP) retreat, which was a life-changing experience for him. Afterward he was excited and renewed in his faith and encouraged Karen to attend the women's retreat the following weekend. During that week Sonny went to the Mayo Clinic for a scheduled appointment and found out that his disease had progressed and that he was now being faced with three choices: dialysis, a transplant, or death. As a family they made the decision to move forward with the transplant. His daughter Robyn was at first considered a suitable donor, but due to some health issues she became ineligible, so Sonny began dialysis and was placed on a donor list instead.

Months later as they were preparing to be on the team for the next CHRP retreat, they received a call that a kidney had been found. They learned that the donor was a 19-year-old young man who had died on Friday, October 13, the Feast of Our Lady of Fatima. Ironically, the wife of the anesthesiologist who was part of the operating team had also been on the women's retreat with Karen, and they had become close friends. Sonny's surgery went well, and he became the third-longest kidney recipient in the state of Missouri, lasting 28 years.

By March of 2012 Sonny was told that he needed a new kidney. During the preliminary testing for the new transplant they discovered an abdominal aneurysm which was very serious, and an operation to remove it was needed first. During the procedure it was revealed that the aneurysm had attached itself to both the spleen and the pancreas, but a world-renowned pancreatic surgeon was operating in the next room and was able to assist. Sonny's doctor said later that it was "God's Providence" that the surgeon was there and a miracle that he survived. Over the ensuing months Sonny continued to deal with many subsequent health issues due to his compromised immune system, so it was not until December 21, 2012 that he finally got his second kidney, and while he was feeling better at first, soon he needed surgery again, this time for parathyroid disease. At one point he even had shingles that presented itself as a ring around the top of the head; truly he was carrying the wounds of Christ in so many ways.

As Sonny continued to recuperate, friends invited he and Karen to visit them in Ft. Myers so he could rest and relax. Shortly after arriving they asked them if there was something special they wanted to do, and being long-time Legatus members they said, "Let's visit Ave Maria!" Together they went to the noon Mass in the Oratory, had pizza at Milano's, and shopped at By the Way of the Family gift shop. They also decided to visit the Legatus office to say hello to the staff, but as they were leaving noticed several condos for sale on the window of the John R. Woods realty office downstairs. They met with Joe Rivera, the realtor, to look just for fun, but due to time constraints they never made it to Del Webb.

After returning to Ft. Myers they began to seriously consider the "possibility" of buying in Florida and looked at several developments around the Ft. Myers area. One morning toward the end of their stay, as they were leaving their friends' home to stay in Naples for a few days, Karen awoke as she heard clearly these words in her heart, "but you never looked at the Ave Maria models." She feels was an inspiration from the Blessed Mother to look at Del Webb. When she told Sonny about this they both decided to revisit Ave Maria again, and this time they went on a tour of the Del Webb development. Returning to their hotel room later, Karen said all they could think and talk about was Ave Maria!

When they went home they told their daughter about the idea of them moving, which made her noticeably sad, so Sonny suggested that she and Karen take a return trip to Ave Maria, which they did together two weeks later. As they were flying home Robyn said to her mom, "Why wouldn't you want to move there!" and gave them her blessing. This was June 2013. At this time they thought Sonny was getting better, but the numerous squamous cell cancers on his face—often the effect of the immune suppressants associated with transplants—were becoming more aggressive and quickly growing. As the result of a PET scan, by September 16 a double surgery was scheduled with a head and neck surgeon who found that the cancer had spread, was malignant, and at stage 4. Sonny given eight to 11 months to live with chemo or four months without, but his body was already too weak to tolerate the chemo.

After receiving the news many people did not want them to move to Florida, but Sonny was still determined. He said that he wanted to move there so they could "immerse themselves in the faith with daily Mass and Holy Hours." Unsure of whether they should also keep the condo in St. Louis, they both decided to take it to prayer and let the Lord make the decision for them. Soon after listing the condo they received an offer by a woman whose name was "Marilyn Will" or, as they saw it, "Mary's Will," and by December 4, 2013 they moved into their new and permanent home in Ave Maria. When they were looking at homes they originally wanted something small, but their grandson insisted on the "bigger one," and with all the family that would come to visit, Karen was glad that they did. The home they purchased was on Victory Lane!

In December, as Karen was shopping at the Secret Ingredient in Ave, Sonny saw a painting of the Blessed Mother on the wall and became very excited, wondering if it was for sale. It didn't quite match Karen's décor, but because of Sonny's response Karen decided to ask Jeannie Weber, the owner, about the painting; Jeannie insisted she take it home and try it. When she presented it to Sonny he had tears in his eyes, recalling that the face on the portrait, as well as the statue of Our Lady of Good Help in the grotto at the apparition site in Wisconsin that they had seen, that both reminded him of the beautiful woman that he passed in a gift shop in Medjugorie in 1992; his recollection was that the woman had suddenly disappeared. They both felt that the painting was a gift from Our Lady, who had come to comfort him.

In January they went to the Oratory's parish office to have Masses offered for friends. The first date that was available, however, was March 4, 2014, which they saw as a great blessing because this happened to be Karen and Sonny's anniversary. As it turns out, this would also be the last time Sonny would leave the house before going into hospice. At 3 a.m. the next morning, Sonny was awakened by a bright light and heard a woman calling him. The next day they called Fr. Mayer, who gave him the sacraments as well as the Apostolic Blessing on behalf of the Holy Father, which takes away total admission and punishment due to sin. This was Ash Wednesday.

The following week, at 3 p.m., as Karen and Sonny were preparing to say the Divine Mercy Chaplet together, Sonny suddenly went into an ecstasy. He said out loud, "Oh, the light! Jesus is coming from the light! Do you see it?" Then he began talking to someone who Karen felt was God the Father about her and the entire family. After a few minutes he turned to Karen and asked her if she would leave him alone, so she went into the other room and continued to pray. After 20 minutes she returned as he told her about the vision he had of a beautiful young woman, around 24 years old, who had come to get him. He asked her, "Do you have the keys?" to which she replied, "Of course I do!" He said nothing more and fell asleep. Later, after Sonny's death, Cardinal Burke, a good and personal friend of theirs, would send Karen a card that referred to "Our Lady Gate of Heaven"; it was Our Lady who visited Sonny and she had the keys to the gate!

A few days later Sonny was moved to hospice in Naples. Between 3-4 a.m. Karen said the Divine Mercy Chaplet and then began to say prayers for the dying. At 4:44 a.m. Sonny took three large breaths and was gone. Karen had a priestly blessing on her cell phone from a good friend, Fr. Paul, and played it over Sonny's body as she motioned the phone into the sign of the cross. Throughout the journey of his earthly life he had suffered with Christ, so now at his death she knew, "If, then, we have died with Christ, we believe that we shall also live with him" (Romans 6:8). Later *that morning Karen returned to Ave in time to go to the noon Mass at the Oratory. As she approached the church she saw the large crowd gathered there; it was the Feast Day of the Annunciation, March 25th. Her eyes met with Fr. Mayer's as they were beginning the procession into the church, and she expressed to him that Sonny had passed. Father remembered him in the intentions that day.*

Sonny always carried the cross well and, because of his positive disposition, should have been called "Sunny" instead. He was genuine and brought out the best in people and even at the end, as he suffered, while many offered prayers for his healing, they were healed instead and came to know the great joy in carrying the cross with him. Karen considers Ave Maria his last gift to her!

(On February 15, 2015, Fr. Cory Mayer married Karen Ruberto and Alejandro Kabiling in the Ave Maria Oratory. Another gift from Sonny and another miracle of Ave Maria.)

In the beginning, many questioned who would live in a place that bordered the Everglades and was without any industry or significant businesses around to support it. The answer to that question continues to evolve as Ave Maria grows today. Ave Maria has attracted a diverse cross section of people from all walks of life. The first residents included families of university professors and staff, but also pilots, writers, financial advisors, school teachers, social workers, business owners, doctors, lawyers, realtors, and retirees. Some worked in Naples, Ft. Myers, and Immokalee, while others were self-employed and worked from home. Several even commuted to places like Miami or Ft. Lauderdale, just to be able to live in Ave Maria.

The developers worked closely with strategic planners and Collier County to attract more businesses to this area, part of the plan for an eastward growth of the county. Even with the downturn in the economy, Ave Maria was blessed that Tom Monaghan had chosen these strong partners (Barron Collier Company and Pulte builders) that shared long-term business stability and had the vision to survive the early economic crisis.

In October of 2013 Arthrex, a world-renowned orthopedic medi-cal-device company, built a 160,000-square-foot manufacturing facility in Ave Maria off Oil Well Rd. Governor Rick Scott and Arthrex founder, Reinhold Schmieding, attended the grand opening for a business that would soon employ 500 people at this location with plans to grow. This was great news for Ave Maria, and with their arrival many individuals and families were attracted who desired this closer location to work, as well as others from the east coast of Florida and other states.

Today many Ave Maria residents are those who live here full time, but also seasonal residents who make this their winter home. For some, what began as a seasonal existence in the beginning soon changed as they sold their homes elsewhere to make this their full-time residence. As is true in much of Florida, everyone is from somewhere else, and in a small town environment such as this neighbors depend on one another for rides to the airport, picking up something in town, as well as extend-ing invitations to each another as well as to the university students and faculty to join them in family celebrations and gatherings.

MICHAEL NOVAK: U.S. AMBASSADOR, AUTHOR, AND THEOLOGIAN

EXCERPTS FROM *THE NATIONAL REVIEW ONLINE*, MARCH 1, 2010: "OUR LADY'S UNIVERSITY, THE CATHOLIC CULTURE OF AVE MARIA"

I have never lived in a more Catholic culture than Ave Maria's—well, maybe once before, in St. Pius X Seminary during my college years at Stonehill College. From my room on the Piazza to the Oratory, embraced by the Piazza like a horseshoe, the distance was about 75 yards, and to the Adoration Chapel on the side of the Canizaro Library, 100 yards. All day and all night, students and staff are found in the latter according to formal voluntary shifts, and as the Spirit moves, a steady trickle all day. On Sundays, some 97 percent of the town goes to Mass, and on weekdays about 65 percent of the students.

What most impressed me, though, was what Dostoevsky called the "humble charity" of those one meets—the good manners, the willingness to help, and even to seek occasions to help. One of the storeowners came out on the sidewalk to ask if she could bring me food or other things from Publix on her trip later that afternoon; two days later, she stopped at Walgreens in nearby Naples for a prescription I needed.

Further, I was invited out to dinner often by faculty members, and rejoiced in the big families a great many had underfoot. I met a lot of holy people. I admired the serious learning of a remarkably committed and self-sacrificing faculty and (according to students) the seriousness and impressiveness of their teaching.

So I must report that I have come to love Ave Maria deeply, and feel a very strong pull to live out my final years in such a place. The Board of Trustees (of whom I am one) does not wish Ave Maria to be a small Christian enclave, a hothouse, but a large, cosmopolitan university, ultimately the size of Princeton. Already the university's students have a proportion from overseas that, at 13 percent, may be among the highest in the land. They already include three or four Muslim students.

As I read Catholic history, every time there is a great work of God in the making, the Prince of Lies sows a cloud of mischief trying to disrupt it. By that sign, Our Lady really wants this university. The Lord has, as is His wont, given it obstacle after obstacle to surmount, just as He set before Our Lady in her own life.

This has been for me a good place to magnify the Lord.

Through the years many well-known guests have been part of Ave Maria: Supreme Court Justice Clarence Thomas; presidential candidate and former Senator Rick Santorum; former Senator Sam Brownback; former Miami Dolphin coach and Tom's good friend, Don Shula; Florida Governor, Rick Scott, and former Governor, Jeb Bush; novelist, Mary Higgins Clark; Irish singer Dana; and the actress Jane Seymor, to name a few.

Ave Maria has also been privileged to host some first-class relics: the knee bone of St. Mary Magdalene (imagine the very knee that kneeled before Our Lord and washed his feet); the elbow bone of St. Jude (the Saint of the Impossible); and a second class relic of St Gianna Molla, the patron saint of mothers, physicians, and unborn children. Other notables that the reader might recognize are: the Official Documenting Photographer for the Shroud of Turin, Barrie Schwortz; *Bella* star, Eduardo Verastegui; a missionary priest fom the Holocaust and apparition site in Kibeho, Rwanda; representatives from the Fr. Solanus Casey Center in Detroit; Fr. Benedict Groeschel; Fr. Mitch Pacwa from EWTN; Bishop Serafim de Sousa Ferreira e Silva, the Bishop Emeritus of Fatima; Archbishop Francis Assisi Chulikatt, the Vatican's personal observer to the United Nations; Cardinal Levada, the former Prefect of the Congregation for the Doctrine of the Faith; Austrian theologian Cardinal Christoph Schönborn; the Archbishop of Boston, Cardinal Sean O'Malley; and the Archbishop of Chicago, Cardinal Francis George. Many other priests, bishops, and cardinals from around the world have also visited and been part of numerous Ave Maria celebrations.

The list continues to grow as residents meet new visitors every day in the Tropical Smoothie, at the Bean, in the grocery store, and in the real estate office. Stories of unexpected meetings are commonplace, and details are relayed, sometimes with such excitement that the listener wonders if some of these visitors could be angels unaware!

Another great asset to Ave Maria is a private Catholic K-12 school that was founded when the town opened in 2007. The Rhodora J. Donahue Academy was named in recognition of Mr. and Mrs. John and Rhodora J. Donahue's generous donation. John Donahue, or "Jack" as he is known by most of his friends, is a longtime friend of Tom's and the person who Tom first spoke to regarding building the university close to Immokalee. Rhodora is Jack's wife and steadfast partner of over 64 years. The 30,000-square-foot K-12 school teaches in the classical Catholic tradition where students are steeped in knowledge and the truths of their faith. Not all the students who attend the K-12 live in Ave Maria, as many travel long distances just to receive this excellent education.

At the Donahue Academy students have the opportunity to attend Mass, have access to the Adoration Chapel, and are taught the scriptures, in addition to a great liberal arts program. The school has several of the Sisters of Mary Mother of the Eucharist teaching students as well as a wonderful complement of faculty and staff. In 2014 their founding headmaster, Dr. Dan Guernsey, was replaced by Mrs. Regina Code, the former principal of St. Veronica Catholic School in Cincinnati, Ohio, as Dr. Guernsey began his new role as Chair of the AMU Education Department. The Rhodora Donahue Academy's enrollment during the academic year of 2013 was 255 students, and it continues to grow.

ANDREW EMMANS: AVE MARIA UNIVERSITY ALUMNI AND RESIDENT

That God is both merciful and a giver of gifts is something of a truism, perhaps, but for my family and me it is a present reality. In 2006, by the grace and mercy of God, I stumbled, "as one untimely born," across the threshold of the Catholic Church. I had converted from the evangelical protestant faith of my upbringing, a "brand plucked from the fire," and now had no idea how to "be Catholic" myself, let alone raise a Catholic family. The conversion process was an exhausting ordeal (as they often are), and the beautiful wife of my youth had yet to follow me into the arms of the Church. I had come home, but the job was by no means finished. The whole Emmans family needed to come home.

Even out in California I had somehow heard that Ave Maria University, Florida, was about to move from its interim campus to a permanent campus, and that there would be a town built around the university, with an ethos compatible with and complementary to that of the university. To a convert who knew few Catholics, who needed a Catholic education, and who did not know how to build a Catholic culture in his home, it sounded like a place too good to be true. Somehow, by the grace of God, I was able to convince my wife to journey out to Florida, ostensibly merely to take two years to finish my university education, but with the wild hope (which I dared not voice) that both my wife and I would fall in love with the town and university, and that she would meet great Catholic wives and mothers, she would convert, and that we would stay in Ave, and that we would raise our children (totaling three at the time) in an environment more conducive to their intellectual and moral development, and to their education in the faith. I, in turn, hoped to dive into the rich heritage to which I had just been introduced, to befriend priests and professors, and to live in a vibrant university community where our newly discovered faith could be more easily nurtured than was possible where we lived in California.

In an act of pure gratuity and grace, God deigned to answer all my wild prayers and hopes. We have lived now for seven full years in Ave Maria, and my wife came into the Church on Easter Vigil of 2010. Four children have been born and baptized in Ave Maria, for a total of seven, and the four oldest enrolled in Donahue Catholic, the local private k-12 school. While Ave Maria is not paradise, nor is it without many of the same faults found in any other community, it is nevertheless our home. And while we are ultimately looking for a "Heavenly City, one not made with hands," Ave has been an indispensable aid and comfort while we remain viatores, journeying to our true home.

The Emmans family will always be grateful to God for those who had the vision and commitment to build the university and the town, and most especially to Tom Monaghan. His act of faith and obedience has paid many dividends already, and although my family's story is but a small and insignificant consequence of his faithfulness, it nevertheless has been to my family and me a priceless gift. "Deus paravit enim illis civitatem." —Hebrews 11:16

There are also numerous students from the community who attend the public school and are bused from Ave Maria to schools that are in close proximity to the area. Many families also homeschool their children and find a great support system here, as well as access to those extracurricular activities that complement their education. Families in Ave Maria come in many shapes and sizes, but for those who are Catholic, having AMU right in their back yard will make it an easy transition to college if they choose to attend there in the future.

The university students are also great role models for these young people and to all those in the community. Many strong bonds have been formed between the students and the residents over the years as they live side by side and sometimes adopt one another as part of their family. Due to their diligent studies, however, during the weekdays students are often spotted going to Mass, the library, or meals, but tend to stay closer to campus. In the evening and on weekends, however, they enjoy many Student Life activities, sporting events, or hanging out at the local hot spots in Ave or visiting the beaches in Naples—only a 40-minute drive away. In the winter this can be a real plus when the temperatures are 80 and sunny almost every day!

In Ave Maria babies are being born and weddings are being performed. However, Ave Maria has not been spared stories of pain, especially when families suffer a loss.

On August 1, 2010, Matthew (Alex) Klucik, the oldest of seven children and son of Laurie and Robb Klucik, died when the car that he was driving left the road north of Emerson Park in Ave Maria and overturned in a canal. He was a recent graduate from the Donahue Academy and was enrolled to begin classes as a freshman at Ave Maria University in just a few short weeks. Alex was a student of Sr. Teresa Benedicta's (Sisters of Mary Mother of the Eucharist), whose assignment of a personal journal was a great gift to the family, revealing to them the deep spiritual growth that had taken place in him since moving to Ave Maria. The death of Alex was tragic and affected everyone in the community.

ALEX OF AVE MARIA: CONTRIBUTED BY HIS FATHER ROBB KLUCIK

We moved to Ave Maria in 2007 confident that the environment would help us to be constantly mindful of "what matters most," and that we would have the mutual support of our neighbors.[2] We sought peer support to live up to our chosen ideals rather than constant pressure to abandon them.

---

[2] "What matters most" is a signature phrase used by Ave Maria Radio personality Al Kresta when referring to the Gospel.

It is unfortunate that people typically "live together failing to recognize what unites us," which ends up "breaking down the bonds of trust."[3] This fosters "a terrible sense of solitude" because we sense we are living "a destiny devoid of all meaning."[4] But this solitude is not present "when we are conscious of the adequate reason for being with others."[5] This consciousness and the resultant unity pervade the Ave Maria community, even as we go about our daily lives with the same distractions and stresses and sins common to any community.

This consciousness and unity became very tangible during a watershed event in August of 2010. The eldest of our seven children, Alex, died in a car accident in town at the age of 19, about three weeks before he would begin classes at AMU. In the midst of this otherwise senseless tragedy the community united to live and witness and taste "the appalling strangeness of the mercy of God."[6] The deepest significance of our Christian faith was suddenly front and center—and facing that reality together was a powerful source of unity for an inorganic community comprised entirely of people with roots in other towns and states.

The remarks delivered at Alex's wake serve as an expression of the profound beauty and importance of our everyday community life in Ave Maria:

Late last year I consciously let go of Alex to release him into his freedom as an adult. I was surprised and delighted by what I came to see: a Christian young man of great maturity and beauty, molded by God through many of you. A person to become friends with, a man to admire and what could make a father's heart sing more than realizing that his son has qualities the father would like to acquire?

---

[3] Giussani, Luigi. The Religious Sense. Ithaca: McGill-Queens University Press, 1997, p.85. Some residents have become familiar with Giussani's writing through the movement Communion & Liberation, which residents Michael & Susie Waldstein (professors of Theology at Ave Maria University) introduced to Ave Maria.

[4] Ibid.

[5] Ibid.

[6] Pakaluk, Ruth and Pakaluk, Michael. The Appalling Strangeness of the Mercy of God. San Francisco: Ignatius Press, 2011. Resident Michael Pakaluk (chair of Ave Maria University's Philosophy department) titled his recent book (describing the life of his late first wife Ruth and including her letters and public addresses) after a phrase from Graham Greene's novel Brighton Rock.

As we have done with all of our children (and even with our-selves) we entrusted Alex to the people of Ave Maria to help us draw our son to seek a life focused on knowing, loving, and serving God so that he might obtain the promises of heaven purchased for us by Christ.

We now entrust Alex to God's mercy, having witnessed in his life bountiful evidence that despite his sins—the remnant of The Fall that is in us all—he was focused on those very things, which are the only things that matter.

Thank you, all of God's people who helped Alex on his jour-ney—and especially all people of Ave Maria, for doing your part. We moved here so that we could have love and support from an abundance of neighbors as we endeavored to help our children (and ourselves) live and die as would-be saints—and for no other reason.

We have great hope that you and we have succeeded in that task (in that duty we have to one another—and to all—as Christians) with Alex.

It did not take a village to help our dear Alex to blossom into a fine young man devoted to Christ—it took the body of Christ that was present to Alex in Ave Maria in all its many forms. A village without a core of Truth could not have done it.

We now are forced to face together the reality of why we all chose to come to this wonderful village of sinners—indeed this "most unique" community—where we grow, learn and play—and—pray (and die!—yes die) together. But it is a powerful chance to dwell on the truth of His promises and the vital importance we all have in one another's lives as we fulfill our call as followers of Christ to sac-rifice for (that is, to love) one another and take every opportunity to urge and encourage our neighbors in our daily struggles to fight sin and embrace the opposite—sacrifice and love for our neighbor all for the greater glory of God.

For three years you all have been doing this for us and our chil-dren and we hope you know we have been trying to do the same for you. We are able to be joyful—as we should be—even in our son's death because of you. In fact, we are joyful due to our son's death, not because we take joy in his departure from this world, of course. But because this tragic loss has allowed us to experience an abun-

dance of love in ways we can't begin to describe.

And so the reason for this community of Ave Maria, the reason we are committed to our faith in Christ, the reason for the Church— namely, the destiny of each man's eternity—this reason is now something we in Ave Maria confront head on. Laurie and I ask ourselves: did we provide our Alex with what he needed so that he would be happy to choose a life aimed at a joyful eternity with the Creator? And the answer is that we provided him with you, our neighbors and friends. And together we encouraged him and challenged him to face reality—the real meaning of life—with vigor and joy and zeal and charity. Together we proposed our faith to Alex by sharing ourselves with him. By giving ourselves to him, by loving him, and Alex accepted that proposal in his own unique way. He gave himself back to us, by loving us—by serving God.

Alex's story is not complete without noting the impact of his theology teacher and spiritual mentor, Sister Teresa Benedicta, O.P., of the Sisters of Mary Mother of the Eucharist. Before sister left Ave Maria for summer break that year, she spent her last hour in town in the Adoration chapel. It was six in the morning on Sunday, which happened to be Alex's regular holy hour. They prayed the rosary together and then as Alex escorted sister to her convent in our neighborhood they exchanged prayer requests. She encouraged him to persevere in faith and then departed for the airport. Several weeks later, after Alex died, we found this entry in the prayer journal he had written during the school year at her prompting:

I am living for eternal happiness, to see God face to face. Isn't that what all humans should be striving for? There is something wrong if we're not. Even if we don't know, isn't it imprinted in man's soul—longing for happiness? …We just get caught up in the secular world. We give up our free will, selling our souls to the secular world. Thus, when we live our lives, we're being slaves and strive for the secular stuff. We don't even realize it… But this is why God puts people into our lives: so we can free ourselves from slavery. But if secular slaves are so stuck in that world and reject help from God, is it safe to say they're hopeless and helpless? No! Hope never fails. The reason being is prayer… now me? I need to detach myself from material things more so than I am. It's slowing down my plan for God, making me more and more not a free man, but a slave. The more slave I become, the more freedom I lose, thus making it harder to find truth. Lord, I pray that I gain more knowledge about you and your works. It keeps me away from sin. Guide me to freedom. Let me not become prideful, but humble as I grow closer to you. Amen.

Our son was privileged to live in a community that nurtured and inspired him to choose to think and live that way. Our family remains privileged to live in the same community. Who could ask for anything more?

CHAPTER TWELVE

The Ripple Effect
(The 70-Year Vision)

"Give and gifts will be given to you; a good measure, packed together, shaken down and overflowing, will be poured into your lap. For the measure with which you measure will be measured out to you!"
LUKE 6:38

Since Ave Maria University's founding people have asked, "Why start a new university?" As we look back, that question can now be answered with confidence. At Ave Maria new leaders are being formed who will make a significant difference in the outcome of tomorrow.

Tom Monaghan was always a numbers guy. His experience of building Domino's made him a forward thinker and someone who planned with an eye to the future and a gifted ability to envision the ripple effect of small decisions. Thus was born Tom's 70-Year Vision for Ave Maria and her graduates. As Tom visited cities across the country, he developed a vision that donors could identify with and be part of. Those who heard it for the first time were stunned by its implications and began to share it with their friends and neighbors as it took hold of their hearts and minds.

Here are some excerpts from those early speeches:

I have had some time to reflect on what Ave Maria might look like in 70 years if we continue to work hard, remain faithful to the

Church and Magisterium, and rely on Our Blessed Mother's guidance. The goal has always been to have excellence in academics, but even more importantly, excellence in spirituality. If the university stays the course, I believe that AMU's impact could be felt not only during our own lifetime but even more importantly during the lifetime of our children and grandchildren.

If the numbers continue to grow, by the year 2078 there will be 4,000 faithful priests, some of whom will already have become bishops; 2,500 Sisters, many of them teaching in Catholic schools around the country; the university will have built an outstanding education program and trained some 12,000 Catholic school teachers, a number that will include 1,500 principals. In addition, AMU will have educated 400 theologians with doctorates, which is more than one for every Catholic college and seminary in the United States. Graduates could include 5,000 honest lawyers added to our society, with many of them becoming judges or pro-life politicians, and 300 alumni working in the media. There will be 40,000 holy, Catholic marriages, and these couples who will be faithful to Humanae Vitae will have a projected 150,000 children, many of whom will become priests and religious as well—the possibility of 500,000 grandchildren. And this is just the tip of the iceberg! With this kind of impact Ave Maria could serve as a role model to other Catholic schools, causing a ripple effect, the kind of ripple effect that could transform our present culture. – Tom Monaghan

From the very beginning AMU has been faithful to the advancement of higher learning according to the principles of *Ex Corde Ecclesiae* and *Fides et Ratio*, which call for a revitalization of education and a renewal of the Holy Spirit in the work of Catholic universities. Committed to these principles, Ave Maria University's Board of Trustees, along with a dedicated faculty and staff, have diligently worked to ensure that students are provided with the very best in academics and given the spiritual formation to grow and develop into outstanding leaders in both their personal and professional lives. When students are able to understand and embrace both the intellectual tradition and profound beauty of their Catholic faith, they see the world and their own path differently.

Campus Ministry, Student Life programs, and service projects are an integral part of this foundation as they assist students in finding the joy in serving others and offer them the opportunity to experience a deeper conversion of finding Christ in themselves. The friendships that are developed during their time at AMU are also an important part of that transformation. These relationships have a lifelong bond as they share a common understanding of faith and a purpose to use their lives in heroic ways to be a light wherever God leads them.

AMU continues to take shape largely due to the financial support and prayers of many people from across the country, but there is still a lot of work to do. Most schools receive the vast majority of their donations from alumni and with their support they have been able to build large endowments to expand their programs and guarantee their futures. Ave Maria is still very new, with young alumni who are just getting started with new careers and families, but their numbers will grow in time. In the meantime AMU has been very fortunate to have many benefactors supporting the school. When asked why they supported Ave Maria before there was a brick or stone in the ground, many offered that they were inspired by the vision of Ave Maria, its significance in preparing the next generation of young people, and they wanted to leave a legacy that could make a difference in their own future and the future of their children and grandchildren.

DR. MICHAEL WALDSTEIN: MAX SECKLER PROFESSOR OF THEOLOGY, AVE MARIA UNIVERSITY

Friends and colleagues often ask me why I decided to join Ave Maria University in 2008. "You have a doctorate from Harvard. You earned tenure at Notre Dame. You were President of a Pontifical Theological Institute in Austria. You have seen the big world and have played with the big boys. Why would you choose a small and obscure place like Ave Maria University?"

My answer surprises them even more. "It is because of the greatness of Tom Monaghan's vision." They are perplexed. "What, the pizza man? A great vision? Come on!"

Then I explain in more detail. Tom Monaghan experienced the internal dissolution of Catholic universities in his work on several Boards of Trustees. It became clear to him that he should sacrifice his great wealth (nobody objects to the use of the word "great" at this point in the argument) to respond to this crisis. He wanted to make a difference for Catholic higher education as a whole. He wished to give a response to the crisis by founding a university that would be academically excellent. It would address the problems at their intellectual root.

The greatness of Mr. Monaghan's vision lies in its simplicity, directness, and focus on essentials: to build an authentically Catholic university that contains (or will eventually contain) all the major disciplines of a modern university, including the natural and social sciences, which are the dominant forces in our present-day culture; to form young people who are able to live effectively as Catholics in critical engagement with modern culture as priests, sisters, university professors, school principals, teachers, and professionals of various kind.

Mr. Monaghan's vision for Ave Maria University echoes the challenge addressed by Pope John Paul II in 1979 to the largest crowd ever assembled in Eastern Europe, a challenge that was the beginning of the end of Soviet domination. "You, men and women, do not live your freedom as strangers in the strange land of modernity. You are the heirs of a tradition that is a treasure, a spiritual enrichment, a great common good. How could anyone throw this good away? Can we refuse Christ and all that he brought into history?" (John Paul II, Sermon on the Krakow Commons, June 10, 1979. Weigel, Witness to Hope, *319.) John Paul II's challenge awoke the human energies that eventually shook the Iron Curtain from its rod, bringing freedom to many nations oppressed by Communism.*

Only the nobility of a great common good can move persons in their full depth to enter the struggle for freedom. This is the power of a great common good: deep within the human heart, in the very freedom of the person, it awakens energies of love, of devotion, of courage, of sacrifice, that go far beyond what individual persons can achieve by themselves.

This is what I saw in Tom Monaghan's vision. This is why I came to Ave Maria University.

In February 2011, after many years of discussions and trying to implement a plan of succession for President Nicholas J. Healy and Tom Monaghan, the AMU Board of Trustees was successful in finding a replacement and hired Jim Towey as the president and CEO of Ave Maria University. Jim served as president of St. Vincent's College in Latrobe, Pennsylvania from 2006 until June 2010. Prior to his role at St. Vincent's he served four years in the George W. Bush administration as the Assistant to the President and Director of the Office of Faith-Based and Community Initiatives. From 1985 until 1997 Jim also served as a legal counsel for Mother Teresa.

When President Towey arrived, Tom retained his title as Chancellor of AMU and remained on the Board of Trustees, but the day-to-day operation of the university was relinquished to Jim as of July 1, 2011. This new structure enabled Tom to spend more time working with university supporters and engage in more public speaking in order to promote awareness of AMU among high school students and potential benefactors.

The inauguration ceremony for President Towey took place on October, 7, 2011, with Bishop Frank Dewane present. At the event, Tom expressed his gratitude to President Healy and his wife, Jane, for their many years of hard work and dedication to AMU since that modest beginning in Ypsilanti. His relationship with the Healys is one that he will always treasure.

In May 2013 Nick Healy, after being approached by a group of "priests, educators, and lay" people in Ireland, to counteract the crisis of faith there, announced that he would be working on a project to build a new Catholic college in Ireland called Newman College. He is the President and CEO. Nick continues to support AMU as a President Emeritus, and he and Jane spend time with their family both in New

Hampshire and with family members who now live in the Ave Maria community.

Starting with only a few dozen students graduating each year at its beginning, by the fall of 2014, with the addition of 390 students in the freshman class, Ave Maria University had grown to over 1,000 students, with 30 majors that included:

Accounting, American Studies, Biochemistry, Biology, Business, Catholic Studies, Classics and Early Christian Literature, Economics, Elementary Education (K-6), Environmental Science, Exercise Science, Finance, Global Affairs and International Business, Greek, Health Science, Health Science Administration, History, Humanities and Liberal Studies, Literature, Managerial Economics and Strategic Analysis, Mathematics, Music, Nursing, Philosophy, Physics, Political Economy and Government, Politics, Psychology, and Theology.

"Tom Monaghan's vision – to create a fresh, faithful voice in Catholic higher education, to become involved in the transformation of the culture and the transmission of the faith to successive generations, is being fulfilled at AMU," said President Towey in the Fall 2014 edition of *Ave Maria University* magazine. The 70-year vision was now more than a look into the future, but had become a reality!

Living out this "awakening" of the human heart and the desire to transform our culture also led to the opening of the *Mother Teresa Project,* which was established with the approval of the Missionaries of Charity to enable students to continue the mission of this soon-to-be recognized "saint" of the Church in loving service to the poor. With his past history with the Missionaries of Charity and also through creative fundraising, President Towey was able to obtain a $2 million, four-year grant that was given to the university from a generous donor; the goal is to educate the students on the life and writings of Mother Teresa, engage them in service work for the poor, respond to the call of Pope Francis to reach out to the suffering humanity among us, and continue the Mother's advocacy for the sanctity of human life and the family. The Mother Teresa Scholar Program was also initiated as part of this project as an opportunity for the students, through service and education, to be recognized by the university. To qualify, students must be in good academic standing, have successfully completed the necessary formation, volunteer locally 50 hours in an approved program, and make at least one mission trip either in the U.S. or in a foreign country. On April 2, 2014 the Mother Teresa Exhibition Hall was opened across the street from the campus for students and visitors alike to learn more about her life. Through the Mother Teresa Project we see the words of the psalmist that were heard those many years before being prophetically being lived out, "the Lord hears the cry of the poor."

PATTI DE FELICE, AVE MARIA RESIDENT: THE BODY OF CHRIST

Sr. Elizabeth of the Trinity took her final vows as a Sister of Charity in the 1970s, but before that she was known as Delores, the third-born child in a family of eight, with her sister Patti born just three years later. She had tried several orders before, but they were never the right fit until she became one of Mother Teresa's sisters and was able to serve the poor. Sr. Elizabeth's vocation kept her mainly in the States; while serving in the Bronx she would walk the streets handing out holy cards and rosaries while sometimes being spit on and verbally abused. Everything that she did was out of love, with Jesus in her heart and a smile on her face. Patti can recall one time she and her husband John were visiting Sr. Elizabeth in Virginia in one of the worst slums in the area, bringing her money, food, and clothing, which they happily gave to the poor. When they made them a simple lunch, Patti asked what they did for food and Sr. Elizabeth replied that whatever was left on the doorstep they gave first to those in need and then to themselves. Patti said when you were with the sisters you felt like you were in the presence of saints. She said they had a childlike quality about them, always joyful but also under strict obedience.

In January of 2013 Sr. Elizabeth was diagnosed with pancreatic cancer, and although they wanted to operate, she said no because she was not finished yet and had work to do. Over the ensuing months she struggled with her disease, and in November 2013 the family gathered around her to say what would be their last good-byes. Sr. Regina, her companion, told them in her last days that sister told her she still felt she had not fulfilled her duties and needed forgiveness, but then said that she was visited by a vision of the Blessed Mother, who opened the door for her to go to Heaven. One of her last requests was to hear the voice of her brother Anthony, and although Sr. Elizabeth could no longer speak she acknowledged that she heard him, and shortly after that she passed.

Sr. Elizabeth died on February 21, 2014, the day of Patti's birthday and the day the Mother Teresa Project Exhibition Hall was dedicated in Ave Maria. After learning of her death Patti visited several of the sisters who were at the dedication to tell them the news, and although they did not know Sr. Elizabeth personally they were full of joy for her.

Patti and her husband went to the noon Mass at the Oratory, which was in Latin that day as Fr. McTeigue the celebrant mentioned Sr. Elizabeth's passing during the prayers of the faithful. As Patti continued to pray for her sister throughout the Mass at the consecration, something miraculous happened. She looked up and standing next to Father she saw Sr. Elizabeth, radiant, smiling, and timeless. She was immersed in a beautiful light, in white robes, but the blue stripes on her habit were no longer there and she no longer carried a rosary. At first Patti thought it was her imagination, so she closed her eyes and reopened them several times, but each time the vision remained. Toward the end of the consecration, however, the vision began to fade, and Patti said she knew in her heart that Sr. Elizabeth was trying to tell her that she was going to Heaven. As the host was raised Sr. Elizabeth was now gone and had become part of the Body of Christ.

The impact of Ave Maria is also being felt economically. The Tucker-Hall economic impact study (Understanding the Economic Impact of Ave Maria, Guy Hagen, *Business Currents*, August 2011) shows that from 2007 to 2010 more than $814 million was invested into building the community: $446 million in nonresidential and university construction; $77 million in residential construction; more than $19 million in architectural, planning, engineering, and professional services; $4.5 in maintenance; and $16 million invested in the Law School, which are only a few of the expenditures.

The effect of that investment was immediately felt in Southwest Florida through the jobs that were created when the university and town were built. The cash investments were made by those companies that supported the project, but indirectly it continues to be felt by those who are benefiting from their presence here. The study shows that from 2007 to 2010 approximately $1.28 billion in sales were generated in Lee and Collier counties as the indirect result of the Ave Maria community. Indirect jobs include a local demand for products and services, vendors, suppliers, and those who are a "feeder system" to the town, and this was only at its beginning. On another level there are those businesses that have also benefited through what the study refers to as "induced impacts," which would include those who profit as the result of this direct and indirect activity, or from the money introduced into the local economy such as restaurants, retail stores, schools, real estate, and more. This impact is especially felt in the neighboring community of Immokalee through the services that Immokalee and the university have jointed benefited from because of the close proximity of one to the other.

BLAKE GABLE: PRESIDENT OF REAL ESTATE DEVELOPMENT, BARRON COLLIER COMPANIES

The vision of Tom Monaghan extends much further than Ave Maria University. It touches lives of working families, active retirees, inquisitive visitors, and diligent students all across the world. From its earliest days of construction in 2006, Ave Maria became internationally known for its pioneering efforts in its combination of responsible land development, city planning, and educational infrastructure. In Collier and Lee counties alone we have realized a $1.28 billion economic impact to date due to the construction and operation of Ave Maria, totaling more than 10,000 direct and indirect jobs. *The university played a very large role in this impact, contributing $300 million to the region's gross domestic product.*

This rapid success in eastern Collier County, the site of Ave Maria, quickly caught the world's attention, and we now attract visitors from all over the globe, from all walks of life.

As the developer of the project, we are proud to partner with Tom and look to Ave Maria as a model for future university-based towns. His ardent enthusiasm and genuine passion for Ave Maria will forever be reflected in its students, residents, and beautiful landscape.

The significance and influence of Ave Maria University is also being acknowledged by those outside of the community, when such notable publications such as *First Things, Newsweek,* and *The Newman Guide to Choosing a Catholic College* have given their endorsements. In November 2010 *First Things* rated Ave Maria University as the "Most Catholic College" in the United States, stating that its academics were superior to almost all other Catholic schools and they found the faith on campus "vibrant." *First Things* spent two years analyzing data and conducting its own survey on more than 2,000 U.S. colleges before reaching its conclusion. In 2010 Ave Maria University also made *Newsweek's* annual list of best colleges as one of the top 25 "Most Desirable Rural Schools" in the nation. The magazine considers such factors as the "quality of education, 'good teaching,' and intelligence of the students" and it includes both secular and private schools in its determination. *The Newman Guide to Choosing a Catholic College* also continues to recommend the university on its list of only 19 Catholic colleges that receive this honor. The Cardinal Newman Society makes these recommendations based on the institution's commitment to teaching the Catholic faith according to the Magisterium of the Catholic Church, something that AMU is obviously greatly committed to. Ave Maria University is also committed to making enrolling there an affordable choice for families who are looking for an excellent education for their student without the higher price tag that so many universities now burden them with.

The combination of an outstanding Catholic university, a surrounding town that has maintained the small town values that so many people are seeking, and the impact that Ave Maria has had on the surrounding communities can only be compared to a "marriage made in Heaven." Where it will be 70 years from now only God knows, but if the vision continues to be sustained we know that it will be richly blessed and multiplied.

CHAPTER THIRTEEN

Sowing the Seeds of Faith

"You did not choose me, but I chose you and appointed you so that you might go and bear fruit, fruit that will last. And so that whatever you ask in my name the Father will give you."
JOHN 15:16

Tom Monaghan came into the world penniless, but a Catholic Christian. When his father died and he and his brother Jim were put into the orphanage he was devastated, but being raised and taught the faith by Felician nuns is now something he views as a gift. His faith was his inheritance and the foundation on which he would build the rest of his life. He also learned that although he lost his own father at a young age, his heavenly Father was always present and *is always faithful.*

Spending his early years in an orphanage, entering the seminary, and even the cross of being sent from one foster home to another were all part of Tom's early dependence on God. As a young boy Tom had no permanent home to speak of but was drawn to Frank Lloyd Wright and architecture because he wanted to build something that stood the test of time. But, God showed him that our souls are where he lives and that our eternal home is far more important than any structure here on earth.

As a young man, as he was doing his soul searching in the Marines, he asked himself the million-dollar question: Does God exist? If He did exist, and he was quite sure He did, then Tom knew that his eternal soul was the most important thing in the world and that he would have to live his life as God intended. He is the first to admit now that he has not always lived his life perfectly, but reflecting back, he can see how God has used everything in his life to become part of the story. Good or bad, successes or failures, if you give it all to Him, then the results are also His in the end.

Tom had a love for learning and for the most part was self-taught. Graduating at the bottom of his class in high school and never getting past his freshman year in college was a humbling experience for him, but now due to God's great Providence he has received thirteen honorary degrees and built a university, not for himself but for the Lord. In the orphanage he was given a work ethic that continued in the foster homes, throughout the Marines, and it became his source of determination and perseverance in everything he did. This desire to work hard produced in Tom the ability to give his all to Domino's and never give up despite the odds that sometimes seemed against him. At Domino's he learned the lessons of risk, recovery, business, and the sin of pride. He experienced the riches in life because of the success of Domino's and achieved many of his boyhood dreams, but God taught him in the end they were all just rags if he remained spiritually poor. As the years went by, many good people came into his life, but he discovered what real love is when he married Margie and had his daughters, as well as the awareness that you will never be poor if you are rich in love.

Throughout Tom's life he has said there has always been that image of the angel and the devil on his shoulder, which is a battle that has been waged against every soul as we make our choices in life and in a future that sometimes seems uncertain. Tom tried to follow the path set before him to the limit of his understanding and always had an "all in" kind of attitude, even when the picture was not clear. But despite his mistakes and with each new challenge, God always managed to put him back in the driver's seat, and through time he developed tenacity for the Lord with a new understanding of what he was supposed to do. Tom believes that one way to find out the meaning of life is to go after what you think has meaning and, in the process, you will find out what really does. In the end he found out that he was happy without anything because he had already been given everything, and he feels privileged to have been given the wisdom to see it.

In 1998, when the sale of Domino's Pizza was made public and the *Detroit Free Press* headline read, "I (Monaghan) Plan to Die Broke," Tom's giving pledge was made public, but it was something that he had already contemplated for many years. It is an irreversible position, but Tom said that if they buried him today he would be satisfied.

This message was brought home in May of 2011 when Tom was invited to a gathering of billionaires in Tucson, Arizona in response to a "Giving Pledge" that Bill Gates and Warren Buffet had made and urged others to follow their lead. They were challenging them to donate at least half of their fortunes to the philanthropic cause of their choice. By this time Tom had already given away 95 percent of his money to build Ave Maria University. He was seated next to Bill Gates, who talked about wiping out malaria, and others shared their stories about donating to everything from medical research to the arts. Tom thought they were all worthy causes but he said there was not one mention of God or eternity. While he was sympathetic to their causes, at least most of them, he couldn't help but think that a person is not going to live forever. For Tom, he looked at the return on his investment and, while one might temporarily save the body, there was nothing that could compare to saving a soul.

By July 2014, after many years of dedicated financial support to AMU, totaling approximately a quarter of a billion dollars, the university stood financially self-sufficient from Tom. He will continue as be a board member, support AMU to the degree that he can, and raise funds for the university, but it is his hope that others will now "capture this great vision" and support AMU into the future. Very few people have the opportunity and ability to start a university, so Tom saw it as an obligation, but he always knew that this was not something that he could do alone.

Since Ave Maria University is just in its infancy, compared to other institutions, it does not have the alumni base that many other universities have; therefore, it will need the help of those who the university considers "Alumni in Faith." Many of these individuals have been with AMU from the beginning, and numerous others continue to join in their support. We often ask ourselves, "What can I do to make a difference in this world that is so devoid of God and heading down such a destructive path?" Ave Maria is the answer.

In the coming years Ave Maria University will continue to need the prayers and financial backing of many, as God calls students here to be part of His Divine Plan of restoration for the world. *If we are faithful, God will be too.* As the university grows she will need to build the buildings, provide the good faculty, and raise the needed scholarships for these students who are God's antidote to a dying world. By supporting these students now and into the future, we can be assured that they will continue to produce the good, strong, and enduring plants that will yield a great harvest of souls! Whether these contributions are large or small, each one is important and has value.

Ave Maria will likewise need students who are heroic in living their lives and are willing to discern what God is calling them to do with those lives. *They are the key and the reason this university exists!* Whether they are called to religious life, married life, or the lay vocation, God is ready to use them. During their time at AMU they will have the opportunity, through prayer and the excellent teaching that they will receive, to be aware of God's will in their lives and then go out and make a difference. This salvific fruit has already begun as AMU graduates have carried those seeds of faith with them in all areas of our society. Education, politics, business, the family, and especially the Church are beginning to feel the effects of AMU graduates, and they are an example to others that with God all things *are* possible!

For others, their journey means calling Ave Maria home. Those who live here come from varying backgrounds, faiths, and destinations, but each with their own unique story. They are young and old, those who have means and those who are looking for meaning. Some come because they want to raise their families here, others to be part of a family. They come to give and to receive, to search and to find.

In the center of the town of Ave Maria there is an Oratory. Not unlike the towns that have been built in the past, but unique to those that are being built today. It is the heart of the community and a reminder that God is at the center of all life. There is a peace here that is felt by all those who enter, locals or visitors alike, because as Tom Monaghan learned, if we have God, we have *Our Father* and *we are home.*

When the beautiful marble depiction of the Annunciation reached its final completion and the last piece of Our Blessed Mother's draped face was placed into the façade of the Oratory, the town and university also had a Mother. *"Behold your mother"* (John 19:27). She welcomes all of her children, and with her motherly gaze from the sculpture, she is a reminder to us that we are cherished and loved. Where ever Our Lady is, Her Son Jesus is. Mary always leads us to Jesus.

From the very beginning the Lord had a plan for His pizza, *Dominus.* Whether we are aware or not, perfect or imperfect, He can and will use us, too, to achieve His Divine Plan if we only follow the example of Jesus, who prayed, "Father . . . Thy Will be done."

Little did Tom Monaghan know when he flipped those first pizzas that the Lord was going to use them to bring about such a great good. From the tomato seeds that were once cultivated and grown in these fields, to being crushed and "delivered" as pizza to countless homes and college dorms, God has now revealed to us His plan and His miracle— to deliver souls to heaven. And this is *Ave Maria!*

Tom Monaghan and President Emeritus Nicholas J. Healy

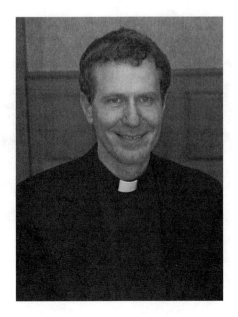

Fr. Joseph Bambenek

Table cloth drawing of Oratory

Beginning construction

Ave Maria - Barron Collier Photo

Sr. Miriam and Sr. Micaela

Jon Scharfenberger and Eric Pfab

Lillian and Dan Bielinski

Maruska Tylsova and Fr. Eamon McManus

Ave Maria Oratory

Crucifix with shadows

Marton Varo - Creator of the Annuciation Sculpture

Fr. Robert Garrity

Alex Klucik Family 2009

Opening of the Mother Teresa Museum with President James Towey

2008 Graduation Photo
of Professors

Graduation 2011

Ave Maria (Hail Mary)

AVE MARIA, gratia plena, Dominus tecum. Benedicta tu in mulieribus, et benedictus fructus ventris tui, Jesus. Sancta Maria, Mater Dei, ora pro nobis peccatoribus, nunc, et in hora mortis nostrae.

Amen